Listen America

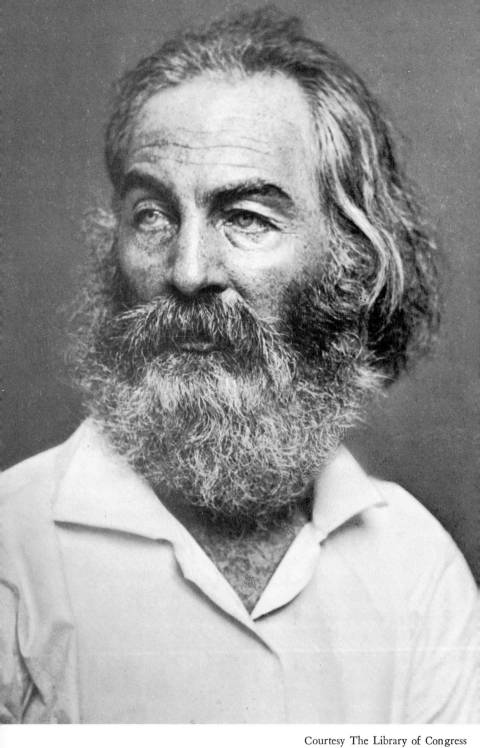

Listen America

A Life of Walt Whitman

ADRIEN STOUTENBURG and

LAURA NELSON BAKER

CHARLES SCRIBNER'S SONS   NEW YORK

Grateful acknowledgment is made to New York University Press, Duke University Press, *American Literature,* and Douglas H. Johnson for permission to quote:

From *The Collected Writings of Walt Whitman,* Vol. 1, edited by Edwin H. Miller. New York University Press, 1966.

From *Faint Clews & Indirections: Manuscripts of Walt Whitman and His Family,* edited by Clarence Gohdes and Rollo G. Silver. Durham, North Carolina, Duke University Press, 1949.

From "Seven Letters of Walt Whitman," edited by Rollo G. Silver. Durham, North Carolina: *American Literature,* Vol. VII, 79, March, 1935.

From *Whitman and Burroughs Comrades* by Clara Barrus. Boston, Houghton Mifflin Co., 1931.

Printed in the United States of America
Library of Congress Catalog Card Number 68-12520

11010

To Gisela Konopka

for her many contributions

toward democracy in the world

Contents

Listen America

1

A Child Went Forth

Regularly each week in the early 1800's, farmers in West Hills, Long Island, could look up from their barns or fields and see a familiar, canvas-hooded wagon loaded with vegetables start off down the road toward Brooklyn. Up front, reins in his hands, sat the equally familiar, plump figure of Major Cornelius Van Velsor nodding a good morning to his neighbors. For years the "Major"—nobody knew exactly how he had got the title—went back and forth between his farm and the village of Brooklyn where he drove his creaking stagecoach onto an East River ferry and took produce across to the markets of New York City.

Very often the aging man had company, a sturdy, black-haired boy who was almost as well known to the Long Islanders as was his grandfather. For the boy, Walt Whitman, had been born in West Hills on May 31, 1819, and even though his parents had moved to Brooklyn when Walt was four years old, he kept coming back to visit the Van Velsor homestead.

The Van Velsors were Walt's mother's parents. They lived two or three miles outside of West Hills and Walt loved the rambling shingle-sided house, the great barn, the sheds and pens, the vast kitchen and fireplace. Most of all he loved the open countryside, the sloping hills from which he could catch glimpses of the sea. Long Island Sound lay only a few miles to the north, and to the south was the gray and blue glimmer of the Great South Bay. The Atlantic Ocean was about fifteen miles away—an easy hike for Walt's strong, young legs—and on still nights he could hear its rustle and boom.

Walt, as the people in the area knew, could turn up anywhere. In cold winters the shallow water inside the outer bars on the bay froze, and there Walt would be with hand sled, ice axe, and eel spear, catching fat eels and filling his basket. In summer he might appear there with his friends to collect the eggs of sea gulls. Whether riding Grandfather Van Velsor's swift horses, digging for clams, or simply sitting dreamily on the seashore, young Walter Whitman was almost as much a part of the landscape as the birds. Not only neighboring farmers but fishermen and cattle drovers, boat pilots and sailors knew him and welcomed him, for even as a youngster Walt seemed to have a special appeal. This was due in part to his appearance, his sun-burnished complexion that set off gray, reflective eyes, but it was chiefly his friendly personality. Around West Hills, or in Brooklyn, the boy could wander anywhere with no feeling of fear. He was a pet of the gatekeepers and deck hands of the ferry boats, and of the stevedores, teamsters, and even the loafers on shore.

It was hard for him to decide which was the more exciting— the Long Island countryside where his father's ancestors had lived since well before the American Revolution, or the noisy, growing village of Brooklyn. Certainly the day he had moved there had been a memorable one in Walt's life. Young though he was, he remembered that jolting thirty-mile trip, the household goods piled in the wagon, and he and his older brother Jesse, and his little sister Hannah, hanging on to the sides. The house his parents rented on Fulton Street was plain and bare, surrounded by taverns and livery stables, slaughter houses and tenements near the waterfront and the United States Navy Yard.

The neighborhood was crowded with workmen like Walt's father.

Walter Whitman, Sr., was a carpenter and house-builder and though he had inherited the Whitman homestead, he had never succeeded in managing either it or his trade profitably. He was a tall, big-boned man of English and Quaker stock, close-mouthed and increasingly bitter over his struggle to make a satisfactory living. Brooklyn, he decided, offered hope of something better, with its growing commerce and its promise of becoming the main port of entry to the United States. In contrast to Whitman's rather morose temperament was his wife's sunny and patient one. Born Louisa Van Velsor, of Dutch and Welsh descent, she had grown up under the influence of her mother's Quaker religion and she, herself, often wore a Quaker bonnet. Years later when Walt was grown and busy "making poems" which were to astonish and even shock many readers of his time, he wrote that his mother's face was "clearer and more beautiful than the sky." Although he felt much closer to her than to his father, his father's liberal attitudes in religion and politics had a strong influence on Walt's own attitudes. All the Whitmans had strongly supported the country's struggle for independence, and Walt's grandfather Jesse Whitman had been a personal friend of the fiery writer of the Revolution, Thomas Paine. Paine was one of Walter Whitman, Sr.'s heroes, as was a preacher, Elias Hicks. Hicks was a leader of the more radical division of the Society of Friends, or Quakers, and an eloquent opponent of slavery. Although Walt's father was not a member of the Friends, nor active in any church, he attended the old but vigorous preacher's lectures whenever Hicks appeared in the vicinity.

Among Walt's earliest memories were the times he accompanied his parents to hear the white-haired preacher. He kept a particularly vivid memory of one occasion, when he was ten

3

years old. Walt's father had come home at sunset at the end of a clear November day, carrying his carpenter's tools plus a load of scrap wood for kindling, which he put down on the floor by the stove.

"Come, Mother," he said to his wife, "Elias preaches tonight."

After a hastily prepared supper, with the young children put to bed—by then Walt had another brother, Andrew, and a baby sister, Mary—Walt and his parents set out for Brooklyn Heights where the richer members of the community had built fine estates. From there it was possible to look across to lower Manhattan Island and see the clusters of ships' masts at the piers; on clear days New Jersey's wooded shores, and Staten Island, were also visible. But in the November darkness through which the three Whitmans traveled to the meeting, only lamps in houses gave a faint glow to the unlighted streets, and the world of river, ship, and bay was a shadowy blur under the stars.

The meeting hall where Elias Hicks was to preach was a dazzling place to young Walt. Glass chandeliers sparkled overhead, the room was furnished in rich, bright colors, and the men and women present were dressed in a variety of costumes. There were fashionable women in silks and feathers, Quaker women in austere bonnets, officers from the Navy Yard in uniform. And, of course, the eighty-year-old Elias Hicks in his black, broad-brimmed hat. Hicks had just returned from a two-year speaking tour which had taken him as far west as Indiana, a long, long way from Brooklyn in that year of 1829. Although Walt tried to keep his mind on the sermon, it drifted to thoughts of the wilderness country—Indiana. The name suggested Indians and the great battles with the red men about which he had read, with muskets and tomahawks, war whoops and trumpets. Though there were fine stands of old trees in the West Hills area, how different the mighty forests of the wilderness must be, and the foaming rivers

—all now being discovered by trappers, boatmen, and settlers who were pushing westward.

On the walk home after the meeting, Walt's mind was still full of wilderness images, but fragments of the preacher's sermon remained. Hicks believed that human beings should make life on earth as full and happy as possible, and that each should follow the inclinations of his own conscience and soul.

Walt was already beginning to follow his inner drives, though he could not express his thoughts in the kind of language Hicks used. At school he was as apt to daydream as study, and although he was good-natured he could be quietly stubborn in following his own pursuits. Public schools were still new in Brooklyn, but Walt was enrolled in one by the time he was six. Schoolmasters were stern, lessons dull, and Walt, drawn by the out-of-doors and by the excitement of city life, often found his mind wandering as he hunched over an uncomfortable, circular desk that served as many as ten pupils crowded together.

In contrast was the excitement of holidays, especially the Fourth of July when the nation celebrated American Independence with parades, speeches, firecrackers, music, and flags. The July 4th celebration in 1825 held an extra interest for six-year-old Walt because on that day one of the great heroes of the Revolution visited Brooklyn. This was the Frenchman, General Lafayette, who as a young man had fought beside George Washington. Walt, standing with other children, watched as Lafayette, his hair now gray, rode up Fulton Street in a yellow coach, waving at the crowds. At Market, Walt and his young companions crowded in behind the carriage and marched with the procession toward a site where a new public building was to be erected. Lafayette was to lay the cornerstone.

Walt's heart thumped to the rhythm of the marching footsteps around him, and his naturally pink cheeks grew even pinker with excitement. When he and the other children reached the place where the ceremony was to be held they climbed to the tops of heaps of earth that had been tossed there by the shovels of workmen who had been excavating the cellar. Men standing below the earth barrier reached up and began lifting the children down to where they could have a safer view of the ceremony. Lafayette joined in, and suddenly Walt saw the famous general standing below him and holding out his arms. Lafayette put his hands under Walt's armpits and lowered him gently to the ground.

When Walt Whitman was an old man, he still remembered that day. He wrote and spoke of it often, and even added that Lafayette had kissed him on the cheek. Whether this last was true or not, being lifted down by the great man was thrilling enough and must have impressed his companions and his family.

There were other excitements in Brooklyn at the time, among them the blowing up of the steam frigate, *Fulton,* named for Robert Fulton, the man who had built the first successful commercial steamboat. The frigate was anchored at the Navy Yard and in June, 1829, was deliberately blown up by a disgruntled sailor. Walt, sitting in school, felt the shock of the explosion ripple through the building and heard the boom. Forty-three persons were killed in the explosion.

A mass funeral was held for the victims and on the day of the ceremony, Walt trotted alongside the marchers in the procession, his emotions stirred by the muffled drums, the bugles playing a dead march, and the sight of sailors marching two by two, hand in hand. The drum beats, mournful music, and the crashing noise of the guns fired in salute at the cemetery recorded themselves in his mind and remained there with all the sounds of ordinary days— the rumble of carts and wagons in rutted streets, the squeal of pigs on public thoroughfares, the creaking of ships moored at the waterfront, the shouts and laughter and curses of laborers, the fights between rival gangs or drunkards, the brash, booming, rustling, and quarreling elements of a village growing into a city. In contrast, there were the quieter sounds of West Hills—the running creeks and songs of water birds, the low sounds of wind in beach grass. Sounds, sights, and smells—Walt savored them all, absorbing them with a kind of greediness, filling himself up. Underneath an outward clumsiness and a lazy, seemingly indifferent manner, there was such sensitivity to everything the outside world offered that he sometimes felt giddy with its abundance.

Yet for all the richness of his inner life, his teachers considered that there was nothing remarkable about Walt, except possibly his rapid physical growth. He attended school for no more than six years; at age eleven he was pushed out into the world to earn his living. Even then he had more education than his father or mother. Louisa Whitman's knowledge of spelling and grammar was poor. Walter, Sr., although he had a small library of books and subscribed to a socialist magazine, *The Free Inquirer,* had very little formal education. None of the family had any great enjoyment of books for their own sakes, so they must have been surprised when Walt became an avid reader.

His first employers, two Brooklyn lawyers who hired him as an office boy, introduced Walt to the delights to be found in reading as well as helping him to improve his handwriting and grammar. When they gave him a subscription to a circulating library, Walt's reading world was expanded still further. He reached out blindly, poring over *Arabian Nights,* the romantic, action-packed novels of Sir Walter Scott, and the early works of James Fenimore Cooper, so that his brain was stuffed with a conglomerate of Sinbad the Sailor, Ali Baba, medieval knights, and American Indians.

At the same time, he had his own daily adventures, such as being sent across the Hudson River by his employers to deliver messages to Aaron Burr. Burr, who had killed Alexander Hamilton in a duel and was later considered a traitor to the Government, had returned from exile in Europe and was living in a house in New Jersey. To Walt, the gray-haired, stately man seemed neither treacherous nor cruel, but gentle and courteous. Burr liked the young messenger, too, apparently, for he often gave him a pear or an apple.

Fruits probably were delicacies in the Whitman household, for the building boom that Walt's father had hoped for did not develop as swiftly as he had expected, and the number of children in the family steadily increased. The Whitmans moved from one house to another in Brooklyn, almost always within the poorer districts. Walt continued to be constantly in touch with laboring men and women: Irish, Dutch, German, Negroes—bargemen, oyster dealers, hucksters, policemen and thieves, firemen and tramps. Street brawls and street parades alternated. Walt was an eager watcher.

In spite of his being attracted to all this and in spite of his rambles through the Long Island countryside, a kind of yeast was working quietly inside the eleven-year-old boy that prevented him from seeing his own future as that of a laborer. When, in 1831, he went to work as an apprentice in the printing office of Samuel E. Clements, editor of the Long Island *Patriot,* his fondness for reading led to an interest in printing and then in writing. The art of printing he learned from an elderly foreman printer, William Hartshorn, who patiently showed Walt how to hold the composing stick and find the letters in the case of type. For "dessert" at the end of the slow process of hand setting the small newspaper, Hartshorn entertained Walt with stories about George Washington and Thomas Jefferson, both of whom he had seen in his younger days. Politics generally was a popular subject among the pressmen and in the front office, too, and Walt's ears were open to all the discussions of Andrew Jackson's presidency and his belief in the common people. The *Patriot* sided with Jackson and his Democratic party, as did Walt's father.

When Jackson was elected for his second term in 1833, he visited Brooklyn, and Walt saw the hardy ex-soldier known as "Old Hickory" ride through the streets in an open carriage, waving his white beaver hat at the crowd, Walt was working as a printer's apprentice for still another newspaper by that time and beginning to attend performances at the Bowery Theatre in New York, using the free tickets passed out to newspaper employees. At first he went with other apprentices his age, but they were bored by such plays as Shakespeare's *Richard III* and were generally so noisy or restless that they ruined Walt's enjoyment. So, increasingly, he went by himself, reaching the theatre early in order to find a good seat in the pit. Shakespeare's lines would sing in his mind for days afterward, even as he read still another romantic novel, or pondered writing a few things of his own.

Although the nation was growing prosperous after a long period of unemployment and business stagnation, Walt's father decided to move his family back to the West Hills area in May of 1833. Either his business judgment was poor, as it so often was—for the building boom he had hoped for in Brooklyn was finally beginning—or else it was a concern for the summer heat and another outbreak of the dreaded cholera epidemic that had occurred the year before. The cholera germs that had raged for centuries through India and then finally followed the trade routes to Europe were brought to America by immigrants from the other side of the Atlantic. In 1832, five thousand New Yorkers died from the disease within a matter of days. Many, especially in the areas where the outbreak was the most violent, fled, leaving possessions and businesses behind them. Those who remained were fearful or in a state of panic. No one knew what caused

9

cholera, and doctors were helpless. One, a Dr. Reese, suggested that it was the indirect result of overindulgence in liquor. It was not until 1884 that Robert Koch identified and described the cholera germ.

Aside from the cholera threat, Mrs. Whitman's health was frail, and she was expecting her eighth child. An infant born several years earlier had died, but even so Walt now had five brothers and sisters. The last two brothers had been given patriotic names —George Washington Whitman and Andrew Jackson Whitman. When the next baby, a boy, was born in the West Hills region home to which the family had moved, he was named Thomas Jefferson Whitman, but was quickly called "Jeff."

Walt remained behind in Brooklyn, making his own way although he was only fourteen. It was not as if he could not visit the Long Island countryside he loved, for Grandfather Van Velsor was still making his weekly trips back and forth. Walt rode with him, enjoying everything except the smell of the lamp black and oil-painted canvas covering the wagon. These made him feel ill, and illness of any kind was an unfamiliar experience to Walt. In heat or cold, rain or sleet, he made his rounds of the piers and streets, creeks and seashore, robust and high-spirited, seemingly impervious to weather or to germs. By the time he was fifteen years old he was as big as a man, tall and stalwart, and handsome enough for strangers to take a second glance at him. But he was still more interested in sailing with fishermen or riding with ferryboat pilots than in fencing himself in by studies or too much industry. His employers on the various papers where he worked found him likable but indolent and busy following his dreams. Although he had not been able to follow Hicks's sermons too well as a child, much of the Quaker's message had penetrated and remained with Walt. God was in everyone, Hicks had maintained, and the Bible was not the final authority. God spoke to the individual man, and it was through an inner light that man should be guided. Each human being was his own holy temple, and if each followed the promptings of his inner voice, men and women could come together in a sharing of faith and companionship. Not only Hicks, but Walt's Quaker background in general, with its emphasis on seeking answers to big questions by meditation and withdrawal, influenced him whether he was conscious of it or not. Already Walt felt a stirring in himself, and a special awareness, even though he could only express it clumsily. He knew that it was there, as was his strong sense of identity with the printers he met, the common laborers on the wharves, the housewives and mothers who toiled in the service of their families. In the latter he saw his own mother, a symbol to him of patience and piety and love. Although he was at an age to be drawn toward girls, he showed little interest in the opposite sex.

Drifter or dreamer though he appeared, he was busy enough. He worked from six to seven hours a day on his newspaper jobs, strove to improve his speaking ability in a Brooklyn debating society, read whatever he could get his hands on, and scribbled little pieces of his own. He wanted eventually to become an editor, and perhaps a writer of successful, popular short stories, to be published in magazines, like those of Nathaniel Hawthorne. At fifteen he had the thrill of seeing some of his work published in a fashionable New York magazine, the *Mirror*. When the mailman delivered the publication to Walt's boarding house, he cut the leaves with shaking fingers, until he found his contribution, after which he read and re-read the words he had written even though his name was not mentioned as the contributor.

He also achieved the first step on his way toward his editorial ambitions, becoming a full-fledged journeyman printer when he was around sixteen years old. Walt went off to New York to work as a compositor in a printing office. New York City was exciting and dangerous, growing rapidly, with thousands of Irish immigrants crowding into it. There were not enough jobs for everyone. Rabble rousers and unscrupulous politicians played on the emotions of the jobless Irish or resentful native Americans so that bloody street fights, riots, and destruction of property were common enough to make it unsafe to walk some of the city streets at night. But it was not this that finally drove Walt back to Long Island. In spite of the social conditions, New York City had the pleasant excitements of theatres, opera, big-sailed packets that plied regularly between the city and Europe, railroads stretching toward increasingly far horizons, steamboats splashing up and down the Hudson, and on the East River the New England schooners. Against the poverty of the immigrants and the unskilled, there was Broadway with its horse-drawn cabs, two-deck buses, pedestrians in silks and ermine, great hotels like the Astor House, showplaces such as Barnum's Museum.

What finally forced Walt to leave the city was a tremendous fire that broke out in the center of the printing, binding and publishing district in August, 1835, followed by an even more destructive fire in December that gutted business buildings in the Wall Street area. A financial depression that had begun earlier deepened, and younger printers were let go. In addition, the winter was so cold that even healthy Walt complained. He went to join his family which had by then moved again, this time to Hempstead.

It was a discouraged Walt Whitman who walked the prairie-like Hempstead plains. His father was trying his hand at farming. Often Walt strolled to the edges of the plains at sundown, watching the large herds of cattle move toward their barns, their tin and copper bells tinkling. Or, for days at a time, he walked

12

along stretches of the island farther east through clumps of pine and scrub oak, wandering the solitary roads, inhaling the wild aromas. There was a growing restlessness in his spirit at the same time that he knew he should settle down to some practical occupation. He could not lean on his family for support. His father had more than enough mouths to feed. Anyhow, Walt prided himself on his self-reliance.

While he tried to decide what step to take next, Walt spent hours with his brothers and sisters, riding young Jeff on his shoulders, taking the six-year-old George with him on short excursions, talking to the girls, Mary and Hannah, or doing what he could around the farm to help out. Walt's mother expected still another child in the fall. Jesse, the oldest, was off to sea and in many ways the household was more peaceful without him, for Jesse had always been strange, excitable, and emotionally unstable. Eight-year-old Andrew, with whom Walt wrestled gently, was sickly and a concern to Louisa Whitman.

Most of all, however, Mrs. Whitman identified with Walt, responsive to the special quality in him that so many others had felt. She observed with a kind of wonder his passion for reading, his scribblings on scraps of paper or in notebooks. Her husband was impatient of his son's dreaminess and lackadaisical attitude toward the farm chores, and especially of his coming and going at all hours according to his own whims. Walt's mother, even though she could never be certain when Walt would appear for breakfast or supper, if at all, forgave him and sympathized even when she could not understand. She saw only that he was troubled, discontented, and seemingly searching. What he might find at the end of his search she could not imagine.

Nor could Walt. Big though he was in body, his mind had not caught up with the emotions and vague aspirations tumbling in him. The words he had put down on paper so far were stilted, artificial, and false. It would be a long while yet before he would write:

> There was a child went forth every day,
>
> And the first object he looked upon . . . that object he became . . .
>
> The early lilacs became part of this child,
>
> And grass and white and red morning-glories, and white and red clover, and the song of the phoebe-bird,
>
> And the third-month lambs and the sow's pink-faint litter,
> And the noisy brood of the barnyard or by the mire of the pond-side,
> And the fish suspending themselves so curiously below there, and the beautiful curious liquid,
> And the water-plants with their graceful flat heads, all became part of him.

Now he was still seeking a way to express himself. Uncertainly, he cast about for some new source of livelihood that would not be completely uncongenial. Perhaps teaching at one of the country schools in the neighborhood would offer both an outlet and a challenge. Such employment required very little except that the teacher know a bit more than the students, and there was almost always a demand since teachers came and went at will. It was worth a try, Walt decided, especially as it would leave him free to roam the countryside.

2

A Wonderful and Ponderous Book

The country schoolhouse at Norwich, a few miles from Major Van Velsor's farm at Cold Springs, was typical of most such schoolhouses of the time, a one-room building with an open fireplace where, if the fire went out, someone had to go and borrow live coals from a neighbor. The teacher at the Norwich School, June, 1836, however, was not typical. Walt Whitman, seventeen, was no younger than many other country schoolteachers, but he was considerably different in his methods and attitudes. It was common for teachers to use a strap or stick to discipline unruly students, but Walt would have nothing to do with corporal punishment. In spite of that, the twenty and more children sitting on backless benches, ranging from five years old to Walt's own age, were well-behaved and paid close attention to the tall instructor. Though there was a faraway look in his blue-gray eyes, and though he sometimes fumbled over words or spellings, he had an air of friendliness combined with authority that drew his pupils to him. Often he would toss aside whatever textbooks there were and teach from his own knowledge. He read poetry to the class, discussed ideas without sermonizing, and was a good storyteller. One of his pupils remembered, "We became very much attached to him. Before and after school and at recess, he was a boy among boys—took active part in games. He had dignity, and yet could descend to sociability, a man out of the average who strangely attracted our respect and attention."

Another pupil had a different impression. "He warn't in his element. He was always musin' and writin' instead of tending to his proper duties."

All his life, Walt Whitman meant different things to different people, for he was not a simple man. "Do I contradict myself?" he once asked. "Very well, I contradict myself. (I contain multitudes.)"

Country schoolteaching was an arduous occupation, poorly paid, and not very highly thought of. At the end of a school day, Walt often felt low-spirited. Long walks over the hills, or riding his grandfather's horses on Saturdays, helped to refresh him, as did chats with the country folk. Moving from one teaching post to another at the end of three-month terms—Babylon, Flushing, Jamaica, and other Long Island villages—boarding with various families, he found himself learning much about human nature. In between teaching terms there was time for talking to farmers and fishermen. At lonely intervals, lying under an apple tree and watching the sky, he let his thoughts drift, wondering about the nature of the universe and his place in it. After the noise and flash, rumble and activity of Manhattan, the country quietness was like a medicine, something he needed for a time. But he could not see himself as a teacher forever. The excitement associated with newspapers and printing shops, politics and parades, pulled at him.

The pull was so strong that in the spring of 1838, when he was nineteen, Long Islanders were surprised to hear that Walt Whitman had been to New York and had come back to Huntington, north of the Van Velsor farm, lugging a printing press and type. The next thing they knew, there was Walt astride a mare, riding around the countryside every week distributing a newspaper called the *Long Islander*. Walt, one way or another, had become both publisher and editor of his own paper. Either he had saved enough from his teacher's earnings to start the venture, or he had succeeded in talking friends into investing in it with him. However he had done it, the farmers and their wives looked forward to the sight of the young man riding jauntily down their country lanes. He, in turn, was enjoying himself and thought he had never had happier moments than when he was trotting to Babylon, down the south road, across to Smithtown and Comac, and back home. The paper was almost entirely his own creation, including the press work, although his young brother George helped out and lived with him in a room over the print shop. In spite of the hours Walt put into the paper, and his desire to make it a success, he would linger in hayfields, talking to "dear old-fashioned farmers," or stop at their invitation for dinner, warming to their hospitality, the sweet evenings in a yard or on a porch, enjoying the sight of the shy, sun-polished faces of the girls. But he never took an interest in a particular girl to anyone's knowledge.

Nor did he smoke or drink, according to friends who used to meet in the shop over the print room to spend an evening with him. He was fond of playing cards and other games. He could enter into a baseball game with enthusiasm but disliked hunting and was not much of a fisherman. Talking and arguments he loved, especially if the talk had to do with politics and the future of America. To him the great destiny of the United States was as real as the sunlight he basked in, and the Declaration of Independence was almost holy scripture. Nothing, he thought, could prevent the forward sweep of progress, not even the existence of slavery in the South. He was against slavery, but the Union came first.

He let his political views and hopes be known through essays and poems in the little *Long Islander* as long as it lasted, which was until the end of the year. Later he said he abandoned the paper because of restlessness—an apparent contradiction to his having said he was happy and content. At any rate, he sold the horse Nina, though he had grown fond of her, closed up shop, loafed for a time with his family, who were now living in Babylon, and set out again for New York, where he hoped to find a good newspaper berth. As an ex-publisher and editor, he expected some respect.

But his journalistic ambitions crashed because of the continuing depression. Back to Long Island he went and found a job in Jamaica writing and setting type for the *Long Island Democrat*. He boarded with the paper's editor, James Brenton, and was not popular with Brenton's wife. "Dreamy and impractical," she complained to her husband, "always underfoot and in the way." Walt, used to dressing in a casual fashion, going about in shirtsleeves if he liked, found himself forced to appear at the Brentons' dinner table in a formal coat, resentfully aware of Mrs. Brenton's sharply watching eyes. He realized that in her opinion he was a loafer.

Nettled, he sat down and wrote an essay for the newspaper on the pleasures of loafing—it was printed only after Walt had left the paper to take up teaching again.

Actually, he was not the loafer he sometimes appeared to be. Aside from teaching, doing odd jobs, writing contributions to newspapers, he was also in the thick of politics. He electioneered for the Democrats, joining in the rough battles of the times, taking to the platform more than once as an official representative of his party. Withdrawn though he was, as some people said, even morose, he was spending himself in many directions and not just lying under apple trees studying the sky. Walt still dreamed of being a journalist and popular writer, but beyond these his brain was filled with something more, some "wonderful and ponderous book," something into which he could put everything, including the whole cosmos if need be.

Near his twenty-second birthday, Walt boarded one of the ferries to New York City, which now was brimming with nearly half a million people, determined again to try his luck there. New newspapers like the New York *Herald,* which James Gordon Bennett had begun in 1835, were prospering, and Walt was no longer a simple journeyman seeking an ordinary job. Leaning on the ferry rail, gazing at the growing skyline of Manhattan, where some buildings were as high as eight and ten stories, he felt a confidence in his talents and in his general knowledge of the "ins and outs" of newspaper work and politics. He was no stranger to the challenging city with its slums, its dock terminals and warehouses, Tammany Hall, the shifting tides of humanity. He had had enough for a while of meadows and cowbells and even of unpressed trousers and shirtsleeves. He glanced down at his neat frock coat, and touched his trimmed dark beard with satisfaction.

Less than two months later, on July 30th, the twenty-two-year-old Walt stood on a platform in the park near City Hall. He was a speaker at the Democratic rally where some twelve thousand persons had gathered. The next day, he had the thrill of finding much of his speech printed in the *Evening Post,* a paper edited by the famous poet William Cullen Bryant.

Walt read the paper in his boardinghouse room and felt his self-confidence surge higher. Politics, poetry, journalism—wherever it was that his "inner light" was directing him, its brightness was beginning to be glimpsed.

What was even more encouraging, he sold his first story to the *Democratic Review,* the outstanding literary magazine then being published. Here, in August, the name of Walter Whitman appeared on the same pages that had welcomed Poe, Bryant, Hawthorne, James Russell Lowell, and James Greenleaf Whittier. Walt's story, called "Death in the Schoolroom," concerned an unsympathetic schoolmaster who beat a frail young student, not realizing the boy was already dead. The editor of the *Democratic Review,* John L. O'Sullivan, a passionate believer in democracy, like Walt, quickly accepted two more stories. The second was entitled "Wild Frank's Return," and related how the hero fled from home because of an over-stern father. Returning home, Frank was accidentally killed by a horse he had been very fond of. The third story also dealt with hostility between a father and son. In this tale, the father's hatred of the son caused him to put the son in an asylum. There the son almost did become insane before escaping. All three stories were heavy-handed and steeped in moral message.

Feeling that he was a successful author at last, Walt began to carry a cane as he strolled down Broadway and to wear a flower in his lapel. He had no way of knowing that posterity would consider these stories, as well as the poems he managed to publish in the same years, hackneyed, sentimental, and without literary worth, though they were no worse than most popular writing of the time. Yet even he must have known that the stories and poems were not the "wonderful and ponderous" book that had tantalized his imagination.

"Shall I, in time to come, be great and famed?" he wrote in one of his early newspaper poems. Certainly he longed to be. His affection for the ordinary man and woman was sincere. But the desire for individual achievement, individual glory, was a driving force. Without some recognition, how could he be sure that the intuition of greatness he had so often felt beside the sea, walking in the wind, looking at the stars, was actual? Shouting it at the sky, confiding it to stones and grass, was no proof.

There were practical matters to contend with. Money for board and room were primary. This meant writing articles and reports for whatever newspaper would buy his work. In February, Walt began writing for a new daily, the *Aurora*. A month later, the publishers announced that "Mr. Walter Whitman, favorably known as a bold, energetic and original writer," was to be their leading editor.

The *Aurora* was very small, but that did not take away Whitman's sense of triumph. The poet in him would have to wait now while he played the role of young editor. In a high hat, frock coat, cane swinging, he strolled in the early afternoons down Broadway to the Battery at the tip of Manhattan, feeling self-important and self-conscious, mocking himself at the same time. Nobody exclaimed, "Oh, there goes Whitman of the *Aurora*!" And the children playing games along the street did not cry out, "There comes a gentleman, we shall have to make way for him." But he continued to act the part of a man of fashion.

Editing, however, with only one reporter to help, was no game. His pen had to scratch away steadily at the Nassau Street office to keep eight or ten compositors busy and do it in time for the paper to be peddled early each morning. After a couple of weeks, he was boasting of the paper's growing success. The *Aurora* would become the most readable journal in the republic, he promised.

Whatever he wrote, article or editorial or essay, his belief in democracy and in the common man remained steady. Not only did he feature articles about ordinary workers such as firemen, drivers, butchers, and peddlers, but he was quick to defend the underdogs of society, striking out in indignation when some fifty prostitutes on Broadway were rounded up by the police and imprisoned in what Whitman considered a "villainous, outrageous and high-handed" way. To the majority of middle-class citizens, there were no lower specimens of humanity than women, no matter how deprived or desperate, who gave themselves to men for money. To Whitman, however, the women were individuals to be pitied and were as entitled to humane treatment as was anyone else.

Many readers were shocked by his articles. Their reaction forced him to admit that perhaps he had used "rather hard words" in denouncing the methods of the police. That was as far as he would go. Principle was more important than popularity or even than his career as editor. And when the *Democratic Review* attacked Charles Dickens' works for presenting so many evil characters, Whitman defended the English novelist who had become one of his favorite writers. Since evil characters did exist, as everyone knew, why shouldn't they be portrayed in literature? he demanded.

Even this was a radical challenge at a time when the official morality, set by the middle-class citizens, decreed that the realities of life, especially those which involved passion between men and women, or a mention of the human bodies hidden within voluminous skirts or men's clothing, should never be discussed in polite society. The "facts of life" were to be kept behind carefully locked doors. Even a simple word like "belch" was too uncouth to be printed. As for the word "sex," the priggish questioned that it should even be in the dictionary.

In May, 1842, the *Aurora* carried a statement saying that Whitman no longer had any connection with the newspaper.

Apparently Walt had been too "bold and energetic" a writer for his publishers, so he had to go job hunting again. If he felt aggrieved, he had the consolation of knowing that he had lasted longer in the editorship than many editors of the time did. Nor did he have to worry long about unemployment. A few weeks

22

later he was made editor of another small daily, the *Evening Tattler*.

This pattern of shifting from paper to paper, in New York as well as on Long Island, was to continue for the next four years. Walt's family, too, shifted their home base so often that they were more like nomads than householders. Walt managed to spend various intervals with them between editorial jobs. He published stories in the *Democratic Review* and even wrote a novel at a time when his funds were low and the cash payment offered was tempting. The novel was called *Franklin Evans, or the Inebriate* and was a fictionalized sermon against the evils of drinking.

The main character in this book is a young man from Long Island, setting out to seek his fortune in New York City, "the great emporium of our western world." On his first night in the city, the rustic adventurer describes himself as "A mere boy, friendless, unprotected, innocent of the ways of the world—without wealth, favor, or wisdom—here I stood at the entrance of the mighty labyrinth, and with hardly any consciousness of the temptations, doubts, and dangers that awaited me there." He does find a friend, but of the wrong kind, and is lured into taking his first drink. "There and then was my first false step. . . ." He becomes a drunkard, tries to reform when he marries a "good woman," but under stress turns again to liquor for comfort.

"About a year after our marriage, the serpent came into our little Eden! . . . I bent beneath the storm, and went back to habits which, until then, my poor Mary had never even suspected. . . ." When he returns home drunk, the shock is too much for his wife and from then on her health fails. "My wife, stricken to the heart, and unable to bear up longer against the accumulating weight of shame and misery, sank into the grave. . . ." Again determined to reform, the narrator wanders to the South where he falls in love with a Creole woman, then later with a blond widow, with fatal results to both women. Back North again, he saves a child from drowning, completely forswears drinking, and is rewarded by inheriting a fortune for his heroism in saving the child.

At the end, Whitman writes, "Reader! I have brought my narrative quite to an end. I may be presumptuous to flatter myself that it has been of much amusement to you, though I had that partly in view. Partly—but not wholly. For I have desired, amid the path we have travelled together, and which is now at an end —that a few seeds of wholesome instruction might be dropped at the same time that we gathered the fruits and the flowers."

Although the novel dealt with a real social problem, drunkenness, Whitman's treatment was so melodramatic and so much more concerned with moralizing than with characters or the art of fiction, it is difficult to believe that the same man who wrote it would eventually become a magnificent poet. The same sentimentality and melodrama appeared in his short stories and poems at the time he wrote *Franklin Evans*.

Certainly the kind of writing he was doing was far from the "wonderful and ponderous" book he had envisioned. What had happened to it and to the drifter and loafer? If riding back and forth on the Fulton ferry, studying the currents and eddies of water, or standing at the Battery watching the boats and splashing tides, or mingling with the Broadway crowds was the role of a loafer, he was still that. And in going from job to job, he was still a drifter. As for the wonderful book, it remained germinating in his mind though he was mostly absorbing the materials for it, occasionally jotting down words or lines in the little notebooks he carried about with him. He continued to educate himself through touch, smell, listening, looking, and also by reading Dante, Shakespeare, Homer, Milton, along with newspapers and magazines from which he snipped whatever might help him become better informed.

In August, 1845, Whitman abandoned the New York scene for Brooklyn. Tammany Democrats had taken over control of the party and since he had opposed them, there was little future for a Democratic journalist in the city. Also, his family had moved back to Brooklyn, and he looked forward to being closer to them, especially his favorite brother Jeff, who was still in school. In Brooklyn he began writing articles for the Long Island *Star* lambasting corporal punishment in the schools, opposing war with England over the dispute between that country and the United States about where the Oregon boundary should be drawn, and giving moralistic advice to youth about the dangers of smoking and alcohol.

In February, 1846, the editor of a rival paper, the Brooklyn *Eagle,* died. The following week Whitman was made the new editor. This became the longest "sit" on an editorial job that Whitman ever had.

In spite of strenuous work at self-education, his grammar was still often shaky—and the *Star*'s editor now mocked him for this. Whitman stabbed back in language that was equally stinging and sarcastic. He was no green journalist, and his years of newspaper apprenticeship had given him a command of journalistic writing that was no handicap.

In his upstairs office, Editor Whitman gave himself whole-heartedly to his new job. The office was his sanctum, which he reached early each morning. There he worked at his desk, interrupted only by visiting politicians or the fifteen-year-old printing apprentice Henry Sutton. "Hen," as Walt called him, recalled many years later that Whitman was a nice, kind man who wore a short beard, was neatly dressed, and had a dignified manner. Often Henry and Walt went together, at the end of the work day, to Gray's Swimming Bath at the foot of Fulton Street. Afterward Walt would board the ferry for New York and ride up and down Broadway on the omnibuses, sitting beside the drivers, sometimes even helping to collect fares. Walt admired the drivers of the omnibuses for their strength and skill in handling their teams of horses, their general lustiness. They welcomed him aboard with a friendly "How are you, Walt?" He knew the name of each driver, names often as colorful as the hard-living and sometimes hard-drinking men themselves; Yellow Frank, Old Elephant, Broadway Jack, Balky Bill. Walt was no drinker, but he was willing to sip a mug of beer with his rough companions, nor did he care if he was criticized for his choice of friends.

Although in his editorials for the *Eagle* Walt urged bachelors and old maids to get married, raise children, and thereby contribute something worthwhile to the nation, he paid little attention to women except to protest the brutal conditions under which female laborers worked, or to praise motherhood. His attachments to omnibus drivers and ferry pilots, and to young Henry Sutton, seemed to take the place of any romantic involvement with a member of the opposite sex. His admiration for "Brooklyn belles" with their "lithe graceful shapes" seemed detached. But he was an ardent supporter of the growing demand by women for equal rights and of social reform in general.

Many changes were taking place in the nation during the year of Whitman's new editorship. Tensions between the South and the North were increasing over the slavery issue. President Polk declared war on Mexico to settle the hot dispute between that country and the new state of Texas over where the boundary should be drawn. All the way west to the Pacific Ocean and south to the Rio Grande, the Texans declared, although the land belonged to Mexico. While United States soldiers marched toward Mexico under General Zachary Taylor, Americans at home fought with words among themselves. Opponents of the war cried that America was undertaking a war of pure aggression. Not so, Whitman responded vigorously. Expansion was part of the nation's destiny, and his imagination burned with the prospect of seeing California and the land of the Santa Fe Trail added to the republic. What, he challenged, did Mexico have to do "with the great mission of peopling the New World with a noble race?" Old "Rough and Ready" Taylor was a hero marching forth to claim land that justly belonged to Americans, Whitman believed along with most of the rest of the nation.

> O resistless restless race!
> O beloved race in all! O my breast aches with tender love
> for all!
> O I mourn and yet exult, I am rapt with love for all,
> Pioneers! O Pioneers!

He had not yet written these words, but this was his mood, which he shared with William Cullen Bryant. America was a shrine at which both worshiped.

With General Taylor winning the war, the big question in 1847 was whether slavery would be permitted in the new territories. Whitman pounded his newspaper pulpit, urging that the Democratic party come out for "free soil," as against slave soil. Slavery should be outlawed in future parts of the Union. Conservative Democrats opposing this stand took over the power in New York State, and the owner of the *Eagle*, under their control, was forced to discharge Whitman from his post.

The new year of 1848 had begun, and once more Whitman was adrift, though not for long. One night in February, Walt was strolling in the lobby of the Broadway Theatre between acts when a man approached him. The man told Whitman that he was planning to start a newspaper in New Orleans with a colleague. Would Whitman be interested in helping the new paper, *The Crescent,* get started? The man, J. E. McClure, said he could offer two hundred dollars down to seal the contract and would pay Whitman's expenses to the southern city.

Walt had no trouble making up his mind. The two shook hands over the deal. The Mexican war was over, and many of the victorious American troops were returning by way of New Orleans, adding extra excitement to the city that had once been the capital of the French colony on the Mississippi. A main port of entry for both cotton and slaves, New Orleans had a reputation for gay living, wickedness, richness and elegance. Just the thought of traveling down the fabulous Mississippi River was enough to set Walt's mind whirling. For the first time, at age twenty-nine, he was to have a look at the world beyond the comparatively narrow confines of Manhattan and Long Island—the mountains, rivers, and forests of which he had so often dreamed.

3

The Endless and Beginningless Road

Two days after being approached by McClure, on February 11th, Walt set off on his new adventure taking his fourteen-year-old brother Jeff with him. Jeff had none of Walt's inward brooding or literary ambitions, but he was vivacious, fun-loving, and Walt enjoyed his company.

Lugging their satchels, they climbed aboard the train in Brooklyn. It was not Walt's first train ride—he had made a Long Island trip by train—but the sight and sound of the steam locomotive puffing out of the station thrilled him. The swaying coaches with their oil-fed lamps, the clack of the rails, the sooty smoke billowing back from the wide-mouthed smokestack— how miraculous was such power and speed, and how marvelous the American ingenuity that had developed it! Ahead lay Baltimore and from there another train journey to Cumberland.

When the two reached Cumberland about sunset a day later, they transferred to a stagecoach loaded with baggage and passengers to cross the Alleghenies. Jolting and swaying, horses straining, the coach set off to climb the steep and rugged eastern slope with no light except that of the stars. All night and the next day the coach rattled onward, stopping only at roadhouses for meals or to change horses. On Sunday night a weary Walt and Jeff crawled down from the vehicle at Wheeling, West Virginia, and made their way to a wharf where their steamboat lay at anchor. It was too dark for Walt to see much of the Ohio River, even if he had the energy to try. He was grateful enough to crawl into bed in a comfortable stateroom and let the captain of the *St. Cloud* attend to the river.

The clang of the breakfast bell awakened the travelers, and Walt and Jeff made their way on deck. After breakfast, Walt had his first good look at the river and got his first jolt of disillusionment. Instead of the flashing stream he had romantically imagined, the Ohio was a mass of yellow brown liquid, the water churning with mud. Nor was the Western breed of passengers around him as noble or heroic looking as he had imagined. At breakfast he had been taken aback by the way the other passengers bolted their food as if the boat and everything on it might sink before they could stuff themselves.

He saw more Western types as the boat steamed on down the Ohio. Many turned out to be roughly clad, some were idlers standing around each landing place. Yet none were the lusty, vigorous giants he had hoped to see. But he told himself that they were probably manlier, basically, than Eastern citizens. He gave himself over to watching the loading and unloading of freight and passengers. Certainly the land was fruitful enough; the *St. Cloud* and other steamers were crowded with cargoes of pork and lard, coffee and flour, bales of leather, dry goods, crates of chickens, turkeys and geese, and even hogs.

After Cincinnati, which Walt decided was the queen city of commerce in spite of its dirty streets, the *St. Cloud* had an adventure which enlivened the sometimes monotonous journey. Just before reaching Louisville, the steamer's captain decided to save time by running the river at that point instead of going through a canal designed to by-pass the dangerous section of the stream. Large rocks and a narrow channel over a rugged stretch of falls extending three miles were real dangers to the vessel even though the captain had lightened it by transferring some of the freight to a flatboat.

Jeff dwelt on the dangers of the adventure in a letter he wrote home. Describing the narrow passageway, he wrote:

> When you get about the middle there is a large rock in this channel, and one on each side of it, the one on the right side is a little distance from the one in the middle, just room enough for a boat to pass through. So you have to take a very sudden turn, or the boat is smashed all to pieces. It happened we got off with a little bump on each rock, we should not have got that (for we had the best pilots that could be found) but one wheel would not work. The fun of the whole thing was, the *fright* we all had, some of the passengers went to bed, others walked the cabin floor, looking as gloomy as if they were going to be hung. Altho I was frightened a good deal, it was not so much as some of the *men* were. If the boat had sunk we were within a few feet of the shore, but I dont think we could have got there, the current was so swift.

Once through the channel, Jeff and Walt could settle down peacefully to the "splendor and comfort" of the steamer, as Jeff described the accommodations. "The greatest of all these splendors is the eating (you know I always did love eating) department." His descriptions of the menus—ham and eggs, beefsteak, sausages, hot cakes, roast beef, mutton, turkey, goose, pies and puddings—certainly suggested that nobody was apt to get thin on the journey.

After twelve days and nights of travel, Walt and Jeff were glad to arrive at the end of their journey—New Orleans. Dirty and exhausted, they hurried to a boardinghouse which turned out to be barely comfortable enough to sleep in. Jeff, already homesick, desperately missed the scrubbed cleanness his mother provided, and he wrote home to tell her so.

After a few days the two Whitmans moved to more comfortable although noisy quarters across the street from the *Crescent* office, and Walt turned to exploring both the city and the problems of his new job. In spite of his being disappointed in the flatness of New Orleans, and shocked at its high prices, he was fascinated by its masses of flowers for sale, the buzzing life of the waterfront, and the busy markets he visited at dawn. At night he wandered through narrow streets, studying the people—soldiers and generals fresh from the war; plantation owners and slaves; rivermen from Kentucky; men and women of mixed Negro, French, and Spanish blood, laughing, loving, and living with a degree of freedom totally different from the Puritan-influenced Yankees in the East. The warmth, the slower rhythms of Southern life, the courtyards shaded by palms, the sound of French spoken by quadroons or Creoles—all were new, strange, and enticing.

Walt put in regular hours at the *Crescent,* going to work early and continuing until eleven at night. Jeff had been hired as office boy and among his duties he had to handle heavy mailbags. Walt worried about this, especially as Jeff was weakened by bouts of dysentery and was hollow-eyed from increasing homesickness. There were no letters from home, although they had begged for news. When Walt finally did hear from his mother, she wrote that there was not enough money to pay the interest on the house mortgage, and he arranged for her to draw from his account at the bank.

At the beginning of his work on the *Crescent,* he had found his employers kind and warm. As time passed, they grew colder toward him, to his surprise and hurt. He never did understand the reason for the growing alienation, nor does anyone else know positively why there was a falling-out. The original bargain had been made hastily, and perhaps Walt's personality or his Northern bias rubbed the *Crescent* owners the wrong way. He seems to have been in the role of a managing editor but was not consulted by his employers as he had expected. Disagreement or misunderstanding about the financial aspects also played a part.

At the end of May, Walt resigned, and he and Jeff started homeward by way of Mississippi and the Great Lakes. On this trip, with stops at St. Louis, Detroit, Chicago, and Niagara Falls, Walt was newly impressed with the variety and richness of what was then the American West. In his notebooks and in his brain he tucked away his impressions, all the shapes, sounds, and scents that he loved as passionately as if America were his bride.

Shortly before he left the *Crescent,* Walt had written what he intended to be a humorous farce about finding his ideal woman at a ball, only to learn that she was married. On the basis of this, and some later remarks by Whitman, a number of biographers invented a love affair between Walt and a beautiful Creole. More recent biographers have dismissed this as imagination. Whitman did claim to have had some "jolly bodily" experiences in the South, but these could have been nothing more unusual than the sensuous delights he always experienced wherever he was. Swimming among breakers, exhilarated by the spume and the hard caress of waves, soaking up sun on a hillside, or even reveling in his daily bath and "currying" his body with a special brush afterward, were "jolly" physical pleasures to him. All of his senses were especially keen, including that of touch. "I believe in the flesh and the appetites," he wrote. "Seeing, hearing, feeling, are miracles, and each part and tag of me is a miracle." The body, he declared, was as beautiful as the soul and no part of it was less beautiful than another. This conviction, growing and deepening in his mind as he grappled with words to express it, was a kind of religion with Whitman. Added to this belief was the immense outpouring of love he felt toward all humanity, from the highest to the lowest, and toward animals and even sticks and stones. It was an indiscriminate, all-embracing desire not only to love but to identify with the loved objects. Looking at hardy young men from Kentucky or Ohio or Manhattan streets, he became those young men in his imagination. Observing slaves in the market, he became those slaves. He indentified with strong, tan-cheeked women, the mothers of what he conceived of as a new race in the world and at the same time imagined himself as husband and father of the new race. He celebrated the love of men for women, but he celebrated also the love of comrades for one another.

He was yet to express these ripening convictions and intuitions in the book that he carried about in his head, and in fact after an apparently drifting summer at home in Brooklyn, he was more concerned with politics and newspaper ambitions than with poetry.

Still battling on the side of the Free Soil Democrats, Walt was put in charge of this faction's paper, *The Freeman*, in the fall of 1848. The day after he moved into his office, a fire raged through the area and burned the office building down with all the equipment and supplies. He managed to start over again two months later, but he was fighting a losing battle against the Democratic leaders who were willing to compromise their principles on the slavery issue in order to keep in power. Since he could not bring himself to side with the other major party, the Whigs, who had scarcely any platform at all except to be against Jacksonism, he was gradually becoming a man without a political home.

As for an actual home, Walt turned carpenter and built a house for himself and his family on a lot he had bought on Myrtle Avenue in Brooklyn. Very likely his brothers Andrew and George, also carpenters, helped out. Because the father's health was steadily failing, the family's support was increasingly the responsibility of Walt and his brothers. The last of these, Edward, born in 1835, would never be able to support himself, as he was mentally defective. At fourteen he could do simple chores such as bringing up coal from the cellar, but he needed supervision even for that. Hannah was still at home to help Mrs. Whitman care for him and the house, but Mary was married, and Jesse was away—perhaps at sea—and was seldom heard from. In the new three-story house on Myrtle Avenue, Walt set up a small printing office and bookstore on the first floor.

Because of ideological conflicts, and growing radicalism on his part, Walt resigned from *The Freeman* in September, 1849. He was not an abolitionist calling for the complete elimination of slavery, since such a demand would split the Union, but he was determined that slavery should not spread. Many others believed as he did, but no effective political party spoke for them. Walt spoke for himself, bitterly, when in 1850 he published a poem in Horace Greeley's abolitionist New York *Tribune,* crying out against those who had deserted the cause of freedom, calling them "Doughfaces, Crawlers, Lice of Humanity . . . Muckworms creeping flat to the ground, a dollar dearer to them than Christ's blessing . . ." Part of his bitter anger was a result of the fugitive slave laws which meant that persons in the North were legally bound to return fleeing slaves to their Southern masters. The same wrath was stirring in the minds and hearts of Whitman's fellow writers of the time, Ralph Waldo Emerson and Henry David Thoreau.

The times were turbulent, but no more so than Walt's thoughts and emotions. The revolutionary movements in Europe had been crushed, and although Whitman declared in another new poem, "Liberty, let others despair of thee, But I will never despair of thee," he felt a deep disillusionment over events abroad and those at home and was driven in upon himself. He had not actually been escaping that self throughout his thirty years, but he had been distracted from work on the great prose poem that had appeared in his imagination. Although on the surface he remained busy with ordinary affairs, dabbling in real estate, building new houses—the family moving from place to place in their old pattern—hobnobbing with a congenial group of artists who had banded together under the name of the Brooklyn Art Union, enjoying the pleasures of Manhattan as before, he was doing some hard thinking. Even while editing the *Eagle* and playing the role of successful man-about-town he had been grappling with disturbing emotions and thoughts.

"I cannot understand the mystery," he jotted down in his notebooks of the time, "but I am always conscious of myself as two—as my soul and I: and I reckon it is the same with all men and women." It is doubtful that the common men and women of whom Walt was so fond felt or thought about themselves having a dual nature. But almost from the beginning, Walt had envisioned himself as a spokesman for the masses. What he felt, they surely must feel; what they felt, he took within himself to try to find expression for. In his boardinghouse rooms in Manhattan, or swimming on a lonely stretch of Coney Island beach, or using his hammer as a carpenter, he committed himself to the common people and to individual liberty. "I will accept nothing which all cannot have," Nor would he identify with intellectuals or money-grubbers. "I will not descend among professors and capitalists—I will turn the ends of my trousers around my boots, and my cuffs back from my wrists and go with drivers and boatmen and men that catch fish or work in the field."

Emerson had looked forward to a new, great poet who would express the democratic, expansionist American spirit. Walt was determined to become that poet. "I will not be a great philosopher, and found any school . . . But I will take each man and woman of you to the window . . . and my left arm shall hook you round the waist, and my right shall point you to the endless and beginningless road." The road of individual discovery, expression, and self-realization.

He would be more than a poet; he would be a prophet. This was his dream. But the first step was to write the poetry. And so, one day, he scratched a motto and a reminder and placed it on his table where he could not avoid seeing it.

The motto said, "Make the Works."

Gone now was the frock coat, high hat, and cane. The poet-laborer, the proletarian prophet, was moving into place, and Walt's clothing changed accordingly. He had been one of the newspaper "boys"; now he was to become one of the "roughs," wearing his trousers tucked into knee-high boots, shirt collar open at the throat, a flannel undershirt showing. He had a flair for dramatizing himself—some critics have called it posing—but what he dramatized at this time was his own inward change.

Make the Works. As far as his brother George could see, he was doing nothing of consequence. "He made a living . . . wrote a little, worked a little, loafed a little. He had an idea that money was of no consequence." In the summer of 1851, Walt spent a couple of months at loafing-working at his sister Mary's house. His outward work was chiefly upon articles about the pleasures of Long Island summer resorts (he was an authority, since he spent much of his time swimming; rambling; eating his favorite food, bluefish; talking with the natives) and pleading for Brooklyn water that was not polluted by "privies, cesspools, sinks and gulches of abomination." Poetry and prophecy could not entirely drag him away from civic interests, and there was plenty of time left over, or simply time stolen, for almost daily trips across the river to Manhattan, to Broadway rides, and the opera.

He was still educating himself, too, pursuing history, studies in comparative religion, and developing a special interest in astronomy. Another interest was a pseudo science called phrenology, much in vogue at the time. Practitioners of the "science" claimed to be able to judge an individual's personality by the contours of the cranium. One of the popular places to have one's head "bumps" studied was Fowler's Phrenological Cabinet on lower Broadway in New York. There, Lorenzo Fowler drew up a chart of Walt's personality. His most prominent characteristics, said the phrenologist, were those of friendship, sympathy, sublimity, and self-esteem. Also, Fowler said that Walt had a grand physical constitution and the power to live to a ripe old age. Further, he was especially endowed with the qualities of "Amativeness" (sexual love), "Philoprogenitiveness" (love of mankind), and "Adhesiveness" (friendship). Whitman was so pleased by the analysis that he referred to it often and even had it published on several occasions.

He spent many hours at libraries in New York, reading and making notes, his interest ranging from the Roman poet, Lucretius, to the political theories of Jean Rousseau or the novels of George Sand. Two of this woman novelist's books were among his most treasured possessions: *Consuelo* and its sequel, *The Countess of Rudolstadt*. He regarded the two as one work, saying, "The book is a masterpiece, truly a masterpiece." Among other British authors, he was familiar with Charles Dickens and Thomas Carlyle. The books of American writers, Washington Irving, Nathaniel Hawthorne, and James Fenimore Cooper, were part of his reading fare, as well as the work of leading American poets. Books that he owned and liked he filled with marginal notes and underscored lines. To further his general knowledge of history, geography, geology, or whatever else caught his interest, he continued to clip articles from newspapers and magazines and pasted them into a scrapbook. Copies of Shakespeare or Homer often traveled with him in his pocket or in his lunch pail. Riding home late at night on the ferry, he entertained his pilot friends by reciting favorite verses or singing operatic arias to the accompaniment of the wave-splash against the keel.

Though he was still in his early thirties, there was already a touch of gray in his black hair. The years were also deepening the lines in his father's face, increasing the moroseness of the aging man's mouth. There was an air of death about Walter Whitman, Sr., which he himself realized. He expressed a desire to return to West Hills and look at the old scenes. Walt went with him. Looking at the familiar buildings and barns, slopes and meadows, remembering the days when his beloved Van Velsor grandparents had been alive, Walt became more aware of how swiftly time passed for all men, including him.

Back in Brooklyn, Walt set to work in earnest on his book of poems, toiling over lines that he had crudely jotted down before, striving with a sense of joy and desperation to write, at last, all that he had thought, felt, and believed, to share it with the rest of the world. He felt like a pygmy with his shoulder under a mountain. Even if he could lift it, even if he could get the words published, would the world applaud him, or laugh? Whatever the result, he must risk everything and express the truth and beauty of the world as he knew it. In the face of hypocrisy, he would hurl his honesty. In the face of prudery and false modesty, he would reveal the realities of the human body—heart, lungs, bowels, nerves, sex organs, disease or health. He would use simple words, the language of the man in the streets. Let the critics and the genteel mock him. But now let them stop him!

Again, to his family, especially the practical George, it seemed that Walt was doing nothing. "He would lie abed late," George recalled, "and after getting up would write a few hours if he took the notion—perhaps would go off the rest of the day. We were all at work—all except Walt."

Page by page, Walt's book grew. Finally, he had twelve completed poems with long and rambling lines. In many, phrase after phrase was separated by rows of dots:

> I hear the bravuras of birds . . . . the bustle of growing
>   wheat . . . . gossip of flames . . . . clack of sticks
>   cooking my meals.

The unrhymed verse form he chose was as free and independent as his own spirit. But lack of rhyme was certainly nothing new. Some of the greatest poetry ever written occurs in parts of the Bible, though the lines are conventionally set up as prose. The book of Job abounds with poetic imagery, and when one arranges the lines into formal lengths so that they "look like" poetry, this becomes more evident to the general reader. God, "the voice out of the whirlwind," challenges Job:

> Hast thou given the horse his might?
> Hast thou clothed his neck with the quivering mane?
> Hast thou made him to leap as a locust?

Shakespeare wrote most of his plays in unrhymed verse. However, he usually employed what is called heroic blank verse, each line following a regular rhythm which in metrics is called a five-foot iambic:

> This above all: to thine ownself be true,
> And it must follow, as the night the day,
> Thou canst not then be false to any man.

One of Whitman's contemporaries, William Cullen Bryant, had achieved fame in 1817 with the publication of his poem, "Thanatopsis," also written with the regular accents and rhythms of blank verse:

> Yet not to thine eternal resting-place
> Shalt thou retire alone,—nor couldst thou wish
> Couch more magnificent. Thou shalt lie down
> With patriarchs of the infant world—with kings . . .

Whitman's poetry lacked the regular meter of such verse, but there was rhythm in his sprawling lines nevertheless:

> Through me many long dumb voices,
> Voices of the interminable generations of slaves,
> Voices of prostitutes and of deformed persons,
> Voices of the diseased and despairing, and of thieves and
> dwarfs,
> Voices of cycles of preparation and accretion,
> And of the threads that connect the stars—and of wombs,
> and of the fatherstuff,
> And of the rights of them the others are down upon,
> Of the trivial and flat and foolish and despised,
> Of fog in air and beetles rolling balls of dung.

Though it was, and is, poetry of a high order, it contrasted sharply with the poetry then in style. One of the most popular and admired American poets of the time was the forty-eight-year-old Henry Wadsworth Longfellow. Longfellow, a Harvard professor with a command of some ten languages, was a man so different from Whitman it was as if they had been born on separate continents. Longfellow's verses were as much a part of upper-class drawing rooms as the furniture. Although he was a skillful craftsman and wrote some poetry that is a part of our literary heritage, much of his work was marred by extreme sentimentality, as in "The Wreck of the Hesperus," or by excessive romanticism, such as that in "The Village Blacksmith."

Longfellow and other poets of Whitman's time embroidered their works with references to Greek and Roman gods, and when they were in desperate need of a rhyme—most of their work was in rhyme—they did not hesitate to twist the normal sequence of a sentence around. "Thy" and "thee" were used a great deal even when the subject was not a religious one, as in Bryant's familiar "To a Waterfowl." Full of overblown language, inverted sentences, with a sermon at the end, it is typical of the poetry of the time. It begins:

> Whither, midst falling dew,
> While glow the heavens with the last steps of day,
> Far, through their rosy depth, doth thou pursue
> Thy solitary way?

In the conclusion we are told that God guides the bird through the sky and protects it from hunters, even as He shelters and guides Bryant, and by implication, all men. Whether one believes this or not, the important thing is that such poems were written and read for their lofty thought and the morals expressed, rather than for the basic beauty of language and re-creation of actual experience.

It was into this kind of literary atmosphere that the earthy, stubborn, self-educated Walt Whitman was planning to launch his own poetry. He had no hope of a commercial publisher taking the book, which he called *Leaves of Grass*, so he would have to scrape together the money to publish it himself. He was not without friends in the printing business. There were the Rome brothers, James and Thomas, with a printing shop on the corner of Fulton and Cranberry. Walt decided to try them, even though they specialized in publishing legal books.

The Rome brothers greeted their friend Walt, looked over the manuscript, discussed business terms and said yes. They would print the book, let him supervise the work, and if he wished, set some of the type himself.

He did wish to. He had always enjoyed handling the slim composing stick and tucking the small pieces of type into their metal forms. Now the pleasure was doubled and tripled, and almost every morning he settled into a special chair at the print shop and hunched over his work after first reading the morning newspapers. Through the spring and into the summer, Whitman worked at the shop. At home, at still a new address, his father lay in bed, paralyzed, and there seemed little hope that he would recover.

Supervising his book's layout, choosing a photograph for the front, fussing over the binding, engraving, size and shape, Walt hoped that his *Leaves of Grass* would bring him both fame and money, money he needed to care for his mother and Edward. It was increasingly apparent that the main responsibility for them would be his.

4

Come Travel With Me

Unnoticed by most people, a small advertisement appeared in the New York *Tribune,* July 6, 1855, announcing that Walt Whitman's poems, *Leaves of Grass,* were for sale at a Brooklyn bookstore at two dollars per copy.

Anyone who bought the book would have received a thin quarto bound in green cloth, the back and front covers heavily ornamented with leaves, buds, and small flowers, the title itself entwined with roots and tendrils. Inside was the engraved portrait of a short-bearded man in a broad hat set at a rakish angle, one hand pushed into the pocket of wrinkled carpenter's trousers, heavy-lidded eyes gazing out.

The beginning of the book was taken up by a long preface. In this, Walt described the role of the poet in America and declared, "The United States themselves are essentially the greatest poem." The ideal poet, he said, must be also a prophet and a seer, with a genius that could match the genius of "the common people. Their manners speech dress friendships—the freshness and candor of their physiognomy—the picturesque looseness of their carriage . . . their deathless attachment to freedom." Describing his own role as poet, he said, "What I tell I tell for precisely what is . . . You shall stand by my side and look in the mirror with me." Finally, Whitman concluded with what was half-plea, half-challenge. "The proof of a poet is that his country absorbs him as affectionately as he has absorbed it."

He was asking more than he knew, for most readers found the long preface strange, with its deliberate lack of commas, and the poetry following it even stranger.

Though there were only twelve poems, they covered some eighty pages. Each poem was untitled so that *Leaves of Grass* seemed to be actually one continuous poem divided into sections. The first and longest poem, later entitled "Song of Myself," began:

> I celebrate myself,
> And what I assume you shall assume,
> For every atom belonging to me as good belongs to you.

If a reader had skipped the preface, he probably would have thought these were the words of a howling egotist. Instead, Walt intended his "I" to speak for all men and women: "I am the poet of the woman the same as the man."

But he departed from this representative role when he introduced his own individual image into the poem:

> Walt Whitman, an American, one of the roughs, a kosmos,
> Disorderly fleshy and sensual . . . . eating drinking and
>   breeding,
> No sentimentalist . . . . no stander above men and women
>   or apart from them . . . . no more modest than im-
>   modest.

The word "breeding" alone, in this context, was sufficient to cause a lifted eyebrow, if not indignation. Certain other passages in the poem seemed more erotic than sensuous, as in his words to the sea:

Thruster holding me tight and that I hold tight!
We hurt each other as the bridegroom and the bride hurt
    each other.

You sea! I resign myself to you also . . . . I guess what you
    mean,
I behold from the beach your crooked inviting fingers,
I believe you refuse to go back without feeling of me;
We must have a turn together . . . . I undress . . . . hurry
    me out of sight of the land,
Cushion me soft . . . . rock me in billowy drowse,
Dash me with amorous wet . . . . I can repay you.

Persons looking for shock could find it. Those in search of awkward phrases, overstatement, and occasional melodrama could find examples of these, too. No great work exists without imperfections, especially no pioneering work that attempts to extend the frontiers of perception and experience. In 1855 it was the exceptional reader of the *Leaves* who could see in the seemingly artless lines the beauty, tenderness, and even grandeur that were there. Nothing was too high nor too low for Whitman's notice. One of the loveliest passages in "Song of Myself" has to do with grass:

A child said, What is the grass? fetching it to me with full
    hands;
How could I answer the child? . . . . I do not know what
    it is any more than he.

I guess it must be the flag of my disposition, out of hopeful
    green stuff woven.

Or I guess it is the handkerchief of the Lord,
A scented gift and remembrancer designedly dropped,
Bearing the owner's name someway in the corners, that we
may see and remark, and say Whose?

Or I guess the grass is itself a child . . . . the produced
babe of the vegetation.

Or I guess it is a uniform hieroglyphic,
And it means, Sprouting alike in broad zones and narrow
zones,
Growing among black folks as among white,
Kanuck, Tuckahoe, Congressman, Cuff, I give them the
same, I receive them the same.

And now it seems to me the beautiful uncut hair of graves.

Tenderly will I use you curling grass,
It may be you transpire from the breasts of young men,
It may be if I had known them I would have loved them;
It may be you are from old people and from women, and
from offspring taken soon out of their mothers' laps,
And here you are the mothers' laps.

This grass is very dark to be from the white heads of old
mothers,
Darker than the colorless beards of old men,
Dark to come from under the faint red roofs of mouths.

What do you think has become of the young and old men?
And what do you think has become of the women and children?

They are alive and well somewhere;
The smallest sprout shows there is really no death,
And if ever there was it led forward life, and does not wait
    at the end to arrest it,
And ceased the moment life appeared.

All goes onward and outward . . . . and nothing collapses,
And to die is different from what any one supposed, and
    luckier.

Lyric passages such as this are interspersed among lines evoking the sounds and sights of cities, crowds, parades, men and women at work. Other passages celebrate the natural landscape with its stars, birds, winds, and animals. Of the city, Whitman writes:

The blab of the pave . . . . the tires of carts and sluff of
    bootsoles and talk of the promenaders,
The heavy omnibus, the driver with his interrogating
    thumb, the clank of the shod horses on the granite
    floor,
The carnival of sleighs, . . .

In another section on the city, he deals only with sounds, beginning, "I hear the sound of the human voice . . . . a sound I love," and continuing,

The ring of alarm-bells . . . . the cry of fire . . . . the
    whirr of swift-streaking engines and hose-carts with
    premonitory tinkles and colored lights,
The steam-whistle . . . . the solid roll of the train of ap-
    proaching cars;

The slow-march played at night at the head of the association,

They go to guard some corpse . . . . the flag-tops are draped with black muslin.

I hear the violincello or man's heart's complaint,
And hear the keyed cornet or else the echo of sunset.

I hear the chorus . . . . it is a grand-opera . . . . this indeed is music!

But he is a lover of the countryside and the wilderness as well, imaginatively joining in the life of farmer, hunter, Indian, settler, wild animal:

Prospecting . . . . gold-digging . . . . girdling the trees of a new purchase,

Scorched ankle-deep by the hot sand . . . . hauling my boat down the shallow river;

Where the panther walks to and fro on a limb overhead . . . . where the buck turns furiously at the hunter,

Where the rattlesnake suns his flabby length on a rock . . . . where the otter is feeding on fish,

Where the alligator in his tough pimples sleeps by the bayou

Over the western persimmon . . . . over the longleaved corn and the delicate blueflowered flax;

Over the white and brown buckwheat, a hummer and a buzzer there with the rest

Where the quail is whistling betwixt the woods and the wheatlot,

> Where the bat flies in the July eve . . . . where the great
> goldbug drops through the dark;
> Where the flails keep time on the barn floor . . .

Thus "Song of Myself" shifts back and forth from scene to scene and voice to voice. "It is you talking just as much as myself . . ." Whitman says. "I act as the tongue of you . . ."

> If you would understand me go to the heights or watershore,
> The nearest gnat is an explanation and a drop or the motion of waves a key . . . .

Some of the finest poetry Whitman ever wrote is contained in this opening poem; excerpts can give only a hint of its quality.

The second untitled poem in the volume, later called "A Song of Occupations," presses nearer to the reader, soliciting his love and attention. "Yield closer and closer and give me the best you possess," Whitman urges.

> I bring what you much need, yet always have,
> I bring not money or amours or dress or eating . . . . but
> I bring as good;
> And send no agent or medium . . . . and offer no representative of value—but offer the value itself.

> The sun and stars that float in the open air . . . . the appleshaped earth and we upon it . . . . surely the drift
> of them is something grand;

Whitman finally launches into some four pages listing and describing all the various occupations and tools of men and women. This cataloging is a mark of Whitman's style. It is impossible to quote the whole section, but a few lines may suggest the method used:

> The currycomb . . the horse-cloth . . the halter and bridle
>   and bits . . the very wisps of straw,
> The barn and barn-yard . . the bins and mangers . . the
>   mows and racks:
> Manufactures . . commerce . . engineering . . the building
>   of cities, and every trade carried on there . . and
>   the implements of every trade,
> The anvil and tongs and hammer . . the axe and
>   wedge . . .

On and on Whitman lists the familiar objects of daily life, even to ". . . the housechairs, the carpet, the bed and the counterpane of the bed, and him or her sleeping at night, and the wind blowing, and the indefinite noises . . ."

The third poem, which Whitman was to call "To Think of Time," is mystical and somber. In it he broods about the inevitability of death for everyone, including himself:

> Slowmoving and black lines creep over the whole earth
>   . . . . they never cease . . . . they are the burial lines,
> He that was President was buried, and he that is now
>   President shall surely be buried.

"I shall go with the rest," he says, but not in fear. With an upswing of mood reflecting conviction, he expresses his belief in ever-continuing life:

> I swear I see now that every thing has an eternal soul!
> The trees have, rooted in the ground . . . . the weeds of
>   the sea have . . . . the animals.
>
> I swear I think there is nothing but immortality!

Poem four, which would be called "The Sleepers," presents the poet as disembodied spirit able to enter into and become one with all various persons sleeping and dreaming, whether in their beds or on battlefields:

> I go from bedside to bedside . . . . I sleep close with the
>   other sleepers, each in turn;
> I dream in my dream all the dreams of the other dreamers,
> And I become the other dreamers.

The sleepers in the poem also include the sleeping dead. "A shroud I see—and I am the shroud . . . . I wrap a body and lie in the coffin . . ." Night becomes a symbol for death, dawn a symbol of rebirth. Though the poet loves "the rich running day," he trusts the night—the night before birth and after death—certain that he will be resurrected from the darkness of time.

"I Sing the Body Electric" was to be the title of the next poem, in which Whitman celebrates the beauty of the human form:

> The bodies of men and women engirth me, and I engirth
>   them,
> They will not let me off nor I them till I go with them
>   and respond to them and love them.
>
> I have perceived that to be with those I like is enough,
> To stop in company with the rest at evening is enough,
> To be surrounded by beautiful curious breathing laughing
>   flesh is enough,

> To pass among them . . to touch any one . . . . to rest
> my arm ever so lightly round his or her neck for a
> moment . . . . what is this then?
> I do not ask any more delight . . . . I swim in it as in a sea.

The poems that follow in the book generally repeat the themes of the earlier compositions. In "Faces," the "sacred faces of infants . . . . the illuminated face of the mother of many children" are contrasted with those that have faces resembling a "milk-nosed maggot" or a "dog's snout." Yet, even in the latter, there are hidden virtues and the hope of redemption. "The Lord advances and yet advances: Always the shadow in front . . . . always the reached hand bringing up the laggards." Another poem, "Song of the Answerer," as it was to be called, repeats the idea of a poet who contains the "answer" to everything, picturing him as a kind of religious savior. A poem eventually entitled "Resurgemus" celebrates the ultimate conquest of liberty over all kinds of enslavement. "Liberty let others despair of you . . . . I never despair of you." The tenth poem, "There Was a Child went Forth," has already been quoted from. Whitman's final, twelfth poem, "Great Are the Myths," is a paean to life and man generally.

It was the first, longer poems that contained most of the material the early readers of *Leaves of Grass* found shocking and even brutish. Along with lines referring to prostitutes, opium eaters, or childbirth, there were many frankly celebrating the body as no less sacred than the soul. "I do not press my finger across my mouth," he wrote; "I keep as delicate around the bowels as around the head and heart . . . . The scent of these arm-pits is aroma finer than prayer, This head is more than churches or bibles or creeds."

This was strong stuff for readers accustomed to Longfellow,

Whittier, or James Russell Lowell, and it undoubtedly would have raised a greater storm than it did if many persons had read it. But Walt's literary bomb fizzled for lack of attention as far as the general public was concerned. He was not alone in being ignored by the people "en masse," as he called them. Herman Melville's masterpiece, *Moby Dick*, one of the most magnificent American novels ever written, had been published four years earlier and had caused scarcely a ripple. Up in Concord, Henry Thoreau, only two years older than Walt, had published the account of his two years in a cabin by a pond. This book, *Walden,* destined to become a classic, was generally disregarded.

Walt's own family paid little attention to his book. George hardly glanced at it, "didn't think it worth reading—fingered it a little." Walt's mother found it completely beyond her. Probably his father never saw the slender volume, for only a few days after it was published, the senior Whitman died.

Walt feverishly sent out review copies to the press and to established authors, including Emerson and Whittier (Whittier, it is reported, threw his copy into the fire), then sat back and waited nervously for the verdict.

The first review, in the *Tribune,* was a friendly one. The language of the poems was "too frequently reckless and indecent," the reviewer Charles Dana said, "though this appears to arise from a naïve unconsciousness rather than from an impure mind." Dana did recognize that a peculiar genius was at work and praised the "vigor and quaint beauty" of certain sections.

Perceptive and sympathetic though the review was, Walt undoubtedly hoped for something more dramatic, whether praise or condemnation. But perhaps even he did not dare to hope for what did occur, the delivery of a letter written July 21st by the dean of American authors, Ralph Waldo Emerson, the famous

"Sage of Concord." Years before, in an essay called "The Poet," Emerson had written about an imaginary, ideal American bard, then had concluded, "I look in vain for the poet whom I describe."

Walt opened the letter, trying to consume the whole at a glance:

> I am not blind to the worth of the wonderful gift of "Leaves of Grass". I find it the most extraordinary piece of wit and wisdom that America has yet contributed. I am very happy in reading it, as great power makes us happy. It meets the demand I am always making of what seemed the sterile and stingy Nature, as if too much handiwork, or too much lymph in the temperament, were making our western wits fat and mean.
>
> I give you joy of your free and grave thought. I have great joy in it. I find incomparable things said incomparably well, as they must be. I find the courage of *treatment* which so delights us, and which large perception only can inspire.
>
> I greet you at the beginning of a great career . . .

It was praise enough to dizzy even a seasoned poet. Surely now, Walt thought, his future was assured. He wanted to rush out and wave the letter in the face of the world, shouting the news. He did the next best thing, carrying it in his pocket, showing it to all his friends and to Dana at the *Tribune,* and allowed it to be printed without even pausing to consider that he should ask Emerson's permission. Nor did he stop there. Emerson's praise should be included in *Leaves of Grass* itself. That could be done only by putting out a second edition, and he immediately began to make plans for it. Let Longfellow and the others maintain their scornful silence. With Emerson on his side, how could he fail? As for certain other reviews that began to appear, he could afford to be indifferent to them, too.

Walt was a scurvy fellow, said the *Criterion*, his mind a mass of stupid filth as if he had the "soul of a sentimental donkey that had died of disappointed love . . . We leave this gathering of muck to the laws which, certainly, if they fulfill their intent, must have power to suppress such obscenity."

Less scathing was *Putnam's Monthly Review*. The editor, Charles E. Norton, called the poems "lawless . . . a sort of excited prose" which he found both preposterous and fascinating. He passed the book on to poet James Russell Lowell, carefully warning him, "one cannot leave it about for chance readers and [I] would be sorry to know that any women had looked into it past the title page."

The Boston *Intelligencer* considered the book a "mass of bombast, egotism, vulgarity, and nonsense," and recommended that "the author should be kicked from all decent society as below the level of the brute. . . ."

In spite of this, American critics generally received the *Leaves* with a surprising appreciation of its literary qualities. Surprisingly, too, the famous Boston clergyman, Edward Everett Hale, although he thought the book "odd and out of the way," defended it against charges of indecency. England reacted with more praise than not, even though *The London Critic* was to declare that "Walt Whitman is as unacquainted with art as a hog is with mathematics."

Although Whitman's beloved masses were unaware of the book's existence, it was circulating better than he knew, thanks in part to Emerson, who thrust the book into the hands of many friends. And, far from Emerson, in Springfield, Illinois, the book had found its way into the offices of two law partners, William

Herndon and Abraham Lincoln. Herndon had left *Leaves of Grass* lying on an office table. His tall partner had picked it up, sat down, and perused its pages for about an hour before he looked up, asked Herndon and a law student present to listen, and began to read aloud. Lincoln responded to the freshness and vigor of the long, rambling lines that were as new in appearance as they were in content. A man of the soil, well-acquainted with the rawness and crudities of frontier life, the twists and depths of human nature, Abe Lincoln was not one easily shocked, although he did think some lines could have been left out. He asked that the book be left in the office, and from time to time he picked it up and in his somewhat reedy voice, again read it aloud to anyone at hand.

Walt was already busy preparing a second edition, and writing new poems or "pieces" as he often called them, to add to the volume. Working at high speed, feeling at the height of his powers, he pushed the book forward. By September he was reading proof on it and hurried the book through the press in 1856.

The new *Leaves of Grass* had a green cover like the first, and though thicker, it was of a size to fit conveniently into a workman's hip pocket. Most important to Whitman, on the book's spine, in bold gold leaf, were the words: "I Greet you at the Beginning of a Great Career/R. W. Emerson." Again, he had not asked Emerson's permission, but seized at this chance to draw attention to his book. It was a high-handed act, but it is possible Whitman did not realize just how much so. Reportedly, Emerson grew colder toward Whitman as a result of this, but not so cold that it prevented him from visiting Walt's home. Walt long remembered Emerson's gentle knock on the door and his first meeting with the man whom he credited with having set him imaginatively "simmering, simmering, simmering before I came to a boil."

In his new edition of *Leaves of Grass,* he included all of Emerson's letter, and added one of his own in anwer. "Here are thirty-two Poems, which I send you, dear Friend and Master . . . I keep on till I make a hundred, and then several hundred—perhaps a thousand . . . A few years, and the average annual call for my Poems is ten or twenty thousand copies—more, quite likely."

These were optimistic words considering that his first edition of one thousand copies had sold very poorly. Actually, it was bluff; Whitman talking aloud to himself and to anyone who would bother to listen. The chance that his second editon would sell any more swiftly than the first was a wishful dream—and in his heart he knew it, in spite of the addition of new poems, among which were some of his best: "Crossing Brooklyn Ferry" (first called "Sundown Poem"), "Song of the Broad-Axe," "Song the Open Road."

Exuberant in his own physical health, he challenged, "How dare a sick man, or an obedient man, write poems?" Robust, convinced of his poetic powers, fiercely independent of the opinions of others, he continued to embrace humanity and nature and the entire cosmos—or "kosmos," as he chose to spell it.

Although Whitman addressed many of his poems to both men and women, his main focus tended to be young workmen. Much of the poetry describing young men was as effusive as the poetry a man might write about physically attractive young women. And in this second edition of his book he openly espouses the phrenological idea of "adhesiveness"—lasting friendship, fraternity, and companionship. At the end of "Song of the Open Road" he uses the Spanish-derived word *camerado*, meaning a close companion, one who shares all:

Camerado, I give you my hand!
I give you my love more precious than money,

> I give you myself before preaching or law;
> Will you give me yourself? will you come travel with me?
> Shall we stick by each other as long as we live?

Because of such lines, but especially because of later poems arranged under the title "Calamus," many persons have concluded that Whitman was a homosexual. Also, he was accustomed to address male friends as "beloved" or "darling" comrades in his letters. Just as often, though, he called them his "darling sons." In old age, he claimed that he had fathered a half dozen children. Whether he said this to counter the accusations of homosexuality or whether it was the truth, is uncertain. It is safe to say that no one knows positively about Walt's Whitman's sex life and probably will never know in spite of all that has been written about the subject.

Love toward the human race he did have in abundance, and he expressed that love in poetry that will last as long as these United States, which he also loved passionately and, during the Civil War, served so well.

"Whoever you are, come travel with me!" he appeals in the second edition of his book.

Some would not. They rejected his sensuous images, his sometimes blatant challenges. "The oath of procreation I have sworn. . . ." Many took such words at their face value. Others saw that what he was "procreating" was himself and his poems and that he never meant his words to be taken literally. Overstatement and understatement are techniques of the writing art. Whitman overstated to the point of effusiveness in his poorer passages and often used exclamation marks unnecessarily.

Underneath the self-proclaimed "rough" was an extraordinary tenderness and delicacy. At the same time, there was an ego so large that it grabbed at every chance to advertise itself, pose in the marketplace, and even praise itself anonymously in reviews of its own work.

"Very devilish to some, and very divine to some, will appear the poet of these new poems," one review read; " . . . an attempt, as they are of a naïve, masculine, affectionate, contemplative, sensual, imperious person to cast into literature not only his own grit and arrogance, but his own flesh and form, undraped, regardless of models, regardless of modesty or law . . . a person singularly beloved . . . by young men and the illiterate . . . not an extraordinary person . . . the begetter of a new offspring out of literature . . ."

This is Whitman speaking about himself!

Still, in the year of 1856, he was not thinking only of himself and his book of poems. Politics was still uppermost among his concerns. The issue of slavery sputtered, burned, and blazed. In spite of laws against them, slave ships still carried their suffering human cargoes into American ports. Whitman seized his journalist's pen again, and wrote an exposé of the slavers. Indignant, also, over the Southern slave owners' determination to force their will on the majority of Americans, he wrote a fiery essay which he subtitled "Voice of Walt Whitman to Each Young Man in the Nation, North, South, East and West," expressing his disgust with the "feeble old men, professional politicians, dandies, dyspeptics" and the like who were ruling the nation. A new political party had been born, in 1854, calling itself Republican, and Whitman felt some sympathy toward it and its candidate, John C. Frémont, the western explorer. But he was not certain that Frémont would be "the Redeemer President." As Emerson had anticipated an ideal poet, Whitman imagined an ideal President.

"I would be much pleased to see some heroic, shrewd fully-informed, healthy-bodied, middle-aged, beard-faced American blacksmith or boatman come down from the West across the Alleghenies, and walk into the Presidency, dressed in a clean suit of working attire, and with the tan all over his face, breast, and arms . . ."

Four years later, a man answering to much of this description would, indeed, become President although he would wear a stovepipe hat and be a rail-splitter instead of a blacksmith.

Whether politicking, "making poems," or singing arias in his bath, Whitman made his regular trips back and forth to Manhattan, hobnobbing with pilots and drivers. Who was that bearded, ruddy-faced man in the soft French beaver hat with tall crown and sweeping brim? passengers sometimes asked.

One of the ferryboat employees on the East River told Walt about the questions. "They want to know if you're a retired captain, or an actor, maybe. Some even wonder if you're a clergyman! Or maybe a smuggler."

Walt laughed, anything but displeased at being noticed by strangers, whatever they thought he was. He was also pleased and flattered when, in the autumn of 1856, two of Emerson's neighbors crossed the river from New York especially to visit him. One was Bronson Alcott, a pioneer in educational reform and father of Louisa May Alcott, who was to become famous as the author of *Little Women*. The other man was Henry Thoreau. On their first visit, Walt was out, and Mrs. Whitman met them at the door and then took them into the kitchen to taste the cakes she was baking. She was sorry that Walt was not home but eager to talk about him, especially about how good he was to her, how wise and well-behaved he had been as a boy, and how the whole family loved him. His brothers and sisters took his advice seriously now that he had grown to be such a great man, she said. When the visitors asked if Walt was still a house-builder, as Alcott had been told he was, Mrs. Whitman said, "Oh, no, his brother is a house-builder, not Walt. He has no business but going out and coming in to eat, drink, write, and sleep."

The two left their calling cards, then returned the next morning. This time Walt met them. He received them kindly, but awkwardly, and led them up two narrow flights of stairs to his attic study. The bed was still unmade, a bed which he shared with his mentally deficient brother, Edward, and there was scarcely any place for the visitors to sit. Walt seemed quite unembarrassed about the roughness of the place, and eagerly answered their questions, even telling them that he bathed daily regardless of winter cold, that he had never been sick or taken any medicine, and that his main interest in life was "making pomes." Having let them into his inner sanctum, he took the pair downstairs. Alcott tried hard to get Whitman and Thoreau into a conversation, but each seemed wary of the other, exchanging polite compliments, but not much more. Thoreau was especially cautious, not knowing what to make of Whitman who was so different from his own reserved, thoughtful self. He was not sure whether Whitman was a braggart and poseur, or an original, new specimen. Whitman, in turn, felt that Thoreau was cold and basically disliked humanity.

He and Thoreau were to meet again and even take walks together. Thoreau warmed to his fellow-writer in time, to the point of saying, "We ought to rejoice greatly in him. He occasionally suggests something a little more than human . . . He is awfully good."

In the meantime, the second edition of *Leaves of Grass* had failed to cause any excitement among readers or reviewers. The author himself was something of a celebrity, but the "hash of mud and gold," as he described his own book, went mostly unread.

There was nothing to do but go back to journalism—and borrow a couple of hundred dollars from a friend in the meantime in order to keep going. In the spring of 1857, Whitman was again an editor, this time with the Brooklyn *Daily Times*.

Sitting at his editorial desk, fighting verbally for civic improvements, exclaiming enthusiastically over the laying of the Atlantic cable, or promoting the construction of a railroad that would stretch from coast to coast, he must often have thought of the failure of his book to be heralded as he had dreamed it would. There were trickles of praise, but where was the great acceptance by the people en masse?

Perhaps, he mused, he should strike out across plain, prairie, and mountain and bring his message to the people in person. He went so far as to draw up a plan for a sweeping lecture tour through the South, the West, and up into "Kanada." He would appear in every city and hamlet, he dreamed, preaching democracy, patriotism, equality, and brotherhood, charging only a few pennies, just enough to cover his expenses.

In his own way, Whitman desired to be an evangelist. As it was, he was a pretty disillusioned, fairly hard-working newspaper hack, struggling to keep afloat economically and yet spare a bit of time to tinker with the poems already published in his book —worrying now about the art of them, the right verb or the right noun—and writing new pieces. Perhaps he could yet grip readers by the throat, hold them, even shake them, and make them listen. For his was a new voice; he knew it, he believed in it.

For the moment and for the next and following issues of the *Daily Times,* he must face current problems. *Why* should there be a city ordinance prohibiting boys from bathing in the river? He could never forgive the policemen who arrested the youngsters. *Why* was it wrong for railcars to run on Sundays? Was it not as good a day as any for people to travel or picnic? And why were certain church pews reserved only for the rich? Weren't the poor as much in need of salvation as the prosperous?

As in many times before, Whitman was still the firebrand going full tilt at windmills that stood in the way of what he believed was progress. The result, as before, was the same. He found himself once again out of a job in early 1859. He was working on a third edition of his poems, hoping to pay for its publication somehow.

He now had a hundred poems ready including those previously printed. "In the forthcoming Vol.," he had written to a friend in 1857, "I shall have, as I said, a hundred poems, and no other matter but poems. No letters to or from Emerson—no quoted reviews. I know well enough that *that* must be the *true Leaves of Grass*."

Let the poems stand on their own feet. Let the book speak for itself.

> Lift me close to your face till I whisper,
> What you are holding is in reality no book, nor part of a book,
> It is a man, flushed and full-blooded—it is I.

5

Foothold in Granite

Rich, hemm'd thick all around with sailships and steam-
ships, an island sixteen miles long, solid-founded,
Numberless crowded streets, high growths of iron, slender,
strong, light, splendidly uprising toward clear skies,
Tides swift and ample, well-loved by me, toward sundown,
The flowing sea-currents, the little islands, larger adjoining
islands, the heights, the villas,
The countless masts, the white shore-steamers, the lighters,
the ferry-boats, the black sea-steamers well-model'ed,
The down-town streets, the jobbers' houses of business,
the houses of business of the ship-merchants and
money-brokers, the river-streets,
Immigrants arriving, fifteen or twenty thousand a week,
The carts hauling goods, the manly race of drivers of horses,
the brown-faced sailors,
The summer air, the bright sun shining, and the sailing
clouds aloft,
The winter snows, the sleigh-bells, the broken ice in the
river, passing along up or down with the flood-tide
or ebb-tide,
The mechanics of the city, the masters, well-form'd, beauti-
ful-faced, looking you straight in the eyes,

Trottoirs throng'd, vehicles, Broadway, the women, the
shops and shows,
A million people—manners free and superb—open voices
—hospitality—the most courageous and friendly
young men,
City of hurried and sparkling waters! city of spires and
masts!
City nested in bays! my city!

Thus, Whitman concluded a poem he called "Manahatta,"
the original Indian name for Manhattan. It is an idealized portrait of the city, for surely not all the citizens had free and superb manners, nor were all the workers well-formed and beautiful. Thugs and thieves were as much a part of the city as were
temperance and abolitionist meetings often accompanied by
riots. The political kettle in 1860 was boiling. In April, the Democrats nominated the "little giant," Stephen A. Douglas, as their
candidate for President. The new Republican party held its con-
vention in Chicago in May, and to the astonishment of the New
Yorkers and the rest of the country, nominated a lean and lank
"dark horse," Abraham Lincoln.

What Whitman's reaction was is not known. Although he was
interested in politics, he was at the time enjoying his role as a
"character" and even a celebrity on Broadway. In a boastful mood
he described himself as the "pet and pride of the Broadway stage
drivers."

This sounds like boyish boasting from a man forty-one years
old, his hair already gray. It was, however, close to the fact. He
was known and liked by four out of five of the stage drivers, and
people generally had begun to stare after him, even those who
still did not know that he had published poetry. His way of dressing made him stand out, together with his commanding air, roll-

ing stride, and his friendliness. He had become, also, a kind of feature of an increasingly popular restaurant run by a German-Swiss named Charles Pfaff. At Pfaff's the so-called Bohemians of the day gathered to sample the proprietor's fine wines and good food at reasonable prices. Writers, artists, actresses, and editors clustered there. Among them was Whitman, long hair streaming behind his ears, a branching beard and mustache, sitting at a reserved, circular table, listening or talking according to his mood, but generally listening. It was at Pfaff's that a young journalist and poet, William Dean Howells, sought Whitman out. "He leaned back in his chair," Howells wrote of their meeting, "and reached out his great hand to me, as if he were going to give it to me for good and all . . . [His] . . . gentle eyes . . . looked most kindly into mine, and seemed to wish the liking I instantly gave him . . ."

For Walt it was a time of high hope and self-confidence. In February of 1860, he had received a letter that was as exciting as that of Emerson's four years before:

> Dear Sir. We want to be the publishers of Walt. Whitman's Poems—*Leaves of Grass*. When the book was first issued we were clerks in the establishment we now own. We read the book with profit and pleasure. It is a true poem and writ by a *true* man.
>
> When a man dares to speak his thought in this day of refinement—so-called—it is difficult to find his mates to act amen to it. Now *we* want to be known as the publishers . . .
>
> We are young men. We "celebrate" ourselves by acts. Try us. You can do us good. We can do you good—pecuniarily.

The authors signed themselves, "Yours Fraternally, Thayer and Eldridge," and gave their address as Boston.

Within a month, Walt was in Boston to draw up an agreement with the young publishers. Almost as soon as he reached there, Emerson called on him. Together the two men walked for a couple of hours in bright, clear weather. Emerson had seen copies of some of the new poems Whitman planned to include in the forthcoming edition of *Leaves of Grass,* and he was worried especially about a group now known as "Children of Adam." These new poems were too bold, Emerson argued. They could damage Whitman's reputation and the sales of the book. He talked on, marshaling every argument he could to persuade Whitman to delete the poems. Whitman felt as if he were under the attack of a commander ordering artillery, cavalry, and infantry against him all at once. He listened and realized that Emerson's arguments were unanswerable; at the same time, however, deep within himself, he believed that he had to pursue his own way.

Finally, Emerson asked, "What have you to say then?"

The bare boughs of large elms made criss-cross shadows over the cold ground, and sunlight highlighted the set of Whitman's mouth. "I feel more settled than ever to adhere to my own theory, and exemplify it," Whitman answered the man he had called "master."

Emerson, clean-shaven except for long side whiskers, a gentleman and aristocrat in dress and manners, did not protest. He accepted Whitman's answer philosophically, and without further argument the two went off to dinner together.

Others were not so calm and philosophic when the third edition of Whitman's book appeared around May of that year. The "Children of Adam" poems concerned the love between men and women. In these poems, Whitman celebrated the perfection of both the male and female form, "the long, sustained kiss upon the mouth or bosom," and hailed "you act divine and you children prepared for, and you stalwart loins." There was another cluster of poems that both shocked and mystified many readers.

This group was called "Calamus." These poems dealt chiefly with "manly affection" and the celebration of the "need of comrades." Often, the lines expressed more than is usually associated with simple friendship: ". . . the one I love most lay sleeping by me under the same cover in the cool night, In the stillness in the autumn moonbeams his face was inclined toward me, And his arm lay lightly around my breast—and that night I was happy." On the other hand, he reached out blindly, seemingly to anyone, man or woman: "Passing stranger! you do not know how longingly I look upon you . . . You grew up with me, were a boy with me or a girl with me . . ." "Friend" and "lover" are used interchangeably, as if it did not matter so long as there existed "The dear love of man for his comrade, the attraction of friend to friend, of the well-married husband and wife, of children and parents, Of city for city and land for land."

Whitman had declared that he would lift the veil from certain realities. In these poems he both lifts and conceals, but a high passion rings through the lines with strong hints of loving someone who did not love him, although it is impossible to know whether he wrote of real loves or of imaginary ones:

> Here the frailest leaves of me and yet my strongest lasting,
> Here I shade and hide my thoughts, I myself do not expose
>   them,
> And yet they expose me more than all my other poems.

Perhaps, but there are as many shadows as lights in these poems.

The greatest new single poem to appear in the volume—and one of Whitman's finest achievements—was one which was later entitled "Out of the Cradle Endlessly Rocking." It was first published in a special 1859 Christmas number of the *Saturday Press,* edited by Henry Clapp, one of the Pfaff group, and was then called "A Child's Reminiscence." This version began:

> Out of the rocked cradle,
> Out of the mocking-bird's throat, the musical shuttle,
> Out of the boy's mother's womb, and from the nipples of
>   her breasts . . .

The music of the first and third lines is rather staccato, abrupt, and the phrase "boy's mother's" is awkward. The rhythm apparently jarred on Whitman's inner ear, for the lines finally became:

> Out of the cradle endlessly rocking,
> Out of the mocking-bird's throat, the musical shuttle,
> Out of the Ninth-month midnight,
> Over the sterile sands and the fields beyond, where the
>   child leaving his bed wandered alone, bareheaded,
>   barefoot . . .

The cradle is now truly rocking, establishing the rhythms that carry through the rest of the poem as the child continues his lonely wandering:

> Down from the shower'd halo,
> Up from the mystic play of shadows twining and twisting
>   as if they were alive,
> Out from the patches of briers and blackberries,
> From the memories of the bird that chanted to me,

From your memories sad brother, from the fitful risings
     and fallings I heard,
From under that yellow half-moon late-risen and swollen
     as if with tears,
From those beginning notes of yearning and love there in
     the mist,
From the thousand responses of my heart never to cease . . .

Throwing myself on the sand, confronting the waves,
I, chanter of pains and joys, uniter of here and hereafter,
Taking all hints to use them, but swiftly leaping beyond
     them,
A reminiscence sing.

The scene changes, focusing now on two nesting birds, male
and female, the boy watching them. And then, in italicized,
briefer lines, it is the birds' voices we hear speaking:

Shine! shine! shine!
Pour down your warmth, great sun!
While we bask, we two together.

Two together!
Winds blow south, or winds blow north,
Day come white, or night come black,
Home, or rivers and mountains from home,
Singing all time, minding no time,
While we two keep together.

Then, suddenly, the "she-bird" does not return to the nest. Perhaps she has been killed, unknown to her mate.

And thenceforward all summer in the sound of the sea,
And at night under the full of the moon in calmer weather,
Over the hoarse surging of the sea,
Or flitting from brier to brier by day,
I saw, I heard at intervals the remaining one, the he-bird,
The solitary guest from Alabama.

The male bird continues to call to his mate, pouring "forth the meanings" which the poet understands:

Yes my brother I know,
The rest might not, but I have treasur'd every note,
For more than once dimly down the beach gliding,
Silent, avoiding the moonbeams, blending myself with the
    shadows,
Recalling now the obscure shapes, the echoes, the sounds
    and sights after their sorts,
The white arms out in the breakers tirelessly tossing,
I, with bare feet, a child, the wind wafting my hair,
Listen'd long and long.

The boy feels both exalted and perturbed by the lament. Is the feathered singer a bird or a demon?

Is it indeed toward your mate you sing? or is it really to
    me?
For I, that was a child, my tongue's use sleeping, now I
    have heard you,
Now in a moment I know what I am for, I awake,
And already a thousand singers, a thousand songs, clearer,
    louder and more sorrowful than yours,
A thousand warbling echoes have started to life within me,
    never to die.

O you singer solitary, singing by yourself, projecting me,
O solitary me listening, never more shall I cease perpetuat-
ing you . . .

He begs for a clue to the meaning of the experience, "The word
final, superior to it all."

Whereto answering, the sea,
Delaying not, hurrying not,
Whisper'd me through the night, and very plainly before
daybreak,
Lisp'd to me the low and delicious word death,
And again death, death, death, death . . .

My own songs awaked from that hour,
And with them the key, the word up from the waves,
The word of the sweetest song and all songs,
That strong and delicious word which, creeping to my feet,
(Or like some old crone rocking the cradle, swathed in
sweet garments, bending aside,)
The sea whisper'd me.

Even before the book containing this exalted and exultant
poem appeared, certain reviewers and critics were sharpening
their verbal knives to attack him. In a daily comic book of the
times, there appeared an eight-line verse calling Whitman's work
obscene. Three lines indicate the tone:

Humanity shrinks from such pestilent reekings
As rise, rotten and foul, from each word, line and page . . .
Which stamp him the dirtiest beast of the age.

Some responsible papers referred to his work as "smut." One reviewer recommended that he commit suicide!

Whitman had assembled a pamphlet quoting critics who had hailed him as a new and powerful poet, but this was not enough to counter the cries of indecency. Back with his family in Brooklyn, Whitman was unable to do more than hope that Thayer and Eldridge would be able to sell enough copies of his book to provide him some royalties. Jesse was finally at home and working in the Navy Yard, still unstable emotionally and mentally. The younger brother, Andrew, was weak from a severe attack of pleurisy. As usual, money was needed and in order to supply it for his family and for himself, Whitman went back to writing for the newspapers.

The nation was in the grip of the political campaign, the parties split among warring factions. The quarreling Democrats were running two separate candidates, the old Whigs supported yet another, and the Republicans rallied behind Lincoln. Slavery was at the heart of almost every speech and campaign, the South muttering threats of rebellion, the North fearing civil war.

In November, Abraham Lincoln was elected President although he received little more than one third of the total popular vote. New York was strongly anti-Lincoln, but Whitman cast his vote for the ex-rail-splitter from Illinois. He believed that Lincoln was the candidate most likely to prevent slavery from spreading to the new territories.

In February, Lincoln passed through New York City on his way to his inauguration. Whitman, a lover of spectacles and parades of any kind, was there. He pushed his way through the silent crowd waiting along the curb. Hailed by one of his driver friends on top of an omnibus that was blocked by the curbstone and the crowds, Whitman scrambled up to the top of the bus and got an excellent view of the avenue leading past the Astor

House where Lincoln was to stay. There was a faint murmur among the people as Lincoln's four-wheeled carriage came in sight. As it drew nearer, the murmur died. The silence was heavy, tense. There had been rumors that the President-elect's life was in danger. South Carolina had already declared that she was no longer a part of the Union, and other Southern states were following her example.

No one knew what to expect, least of all Whitman. In the deep hush, the poet watched as Lincoln stepped down from the carriage. Dressed completely in black, a tall hat pushed back on his head, he stood looking at the crowd with perfect composure. Whitman had a direct view of the "dark-brown complexion, seamed and wrinkled yet canny-looking face, black bushy head of hair, disproportionately long neck," and the cool way Lincoln folded his hands behind his back and gazed with curiosity at the equally curious crowd of faces before him. Then with a stretch or two of his long arms and legs, Lincoln and his attendants walked slowly into the hotel and disappeared.

Was this the "Redeemer President" that Whitman had envisioned earlier? He could not be certain, but he was stirred by the look of the man. If any human being could restrain the newly-formed Confederacy, perhaps that tall, strange figure might.

Less than two months later, on April 13, 1861, Whitman was walking down Broadway around midnight, operatic airs still ringing in his ears, when he heard the cries of newsboys in the distance. He paused; down the dimly lighted streets, the figures of several "newsies" were racing along the pavement, waving papers, and shouting, "Extra-a-a! Extr-a-a!"

Whitman bought a paper from the nearest boy and strode across to the Metropolitan Hotel, where great lamps were still blazing. Other late pedestrians had already gathered there holding their papers up to the light to read the headlines. One glance was enough. Yesterday, the Confederacy had fired upon Fort Sumter, an island fortification in the harbor of Charleston, South Carolina. The United States government had tried to furnish food supplies to the national troops stationed there. This the Confederates regarded as an act of war, since they had demanded the island's surrender, and their gunners had unleashed their fire.

Persons without newspapers crowded around, crying, "What is it? What's the news?"

A man near Whitman began to read aloud. The listeners huddled into silence, disbelief uppermost on their faces. Nobody had thought it would really happen. War. War between fellow Americans, the Union split into two raw and wrestling halves. There were a few mutters of "Treason!", some fists shaken, but for the most part there was silence, almost an inability to know how to react. The crowd of thirty or forty persons stood around a minute or two and then dispersed.

The river, the sky, the glitter of ship lights and house lamps seemed neither so bright nor so beautiful as usual to the bearded poet riding homeward that night. In "Song of Myself" he had written, "My foothold is tenon'd and mortis'd in granite, I laugh at what you call dissolution, And I know the amplitude of time." The granite he referred to had been only partly a symbol of his belief in his poetry. However fractured or rough in parts, its pinnacles would endure. Yet his belief in himself was bound up with his belief in the nation. The United States was the basic granite out of which the "noble, new race," with himself as its spokesman, was to grow. Not that granite was split, might even shatter. This dissolution was not one he could laugh at. As for the amplitude of time, it remained to be seen if time was ample enough to mend what was now shifting and rending apart.

He thought again of the new President scarcely in office. Now would be the test of Lincoln's solemn promise to maintain the Union.

Two days later Lincoln issued a proclamation calling for seventy-five thousand volunteers. It was a small number, but Lincoln, like many others, hoped that the crisis would blow over with a minimum of bloodshed, and a quick victory for the North.

George Whitman was one of the first to volunteer. At the time, he thought he would be serving for a very short term. Then, on July 21st, came the first battle on the field of Bull Run in northern Virginia—a disastrous rout of the Union soldiers. The next day the defeated men began pouring into Washington under a steadily falling rain, banners drooping, faces and clothing dripping with mud. Hastily trained, pushed into battle by the public cries of "On to Richmond!" they returned to a city and a government hardly knowing how to cope with them or the military crisis.

A heartsick Whitman wrote, "The worst is not only imminent, but already here. In a few hours—perhaps before the next meal —the secesh generals [Southern generals], with their victorious hordes, will be upon us. The dream of humanity, the vaunted Union we thought so strong, so impregnable,—lo! it seems already smashed like a china plate. Those white palaces—the dome-crowned capitol there on the hill, so stately over the trees— shall they be left—or destroyed first?" For there were strong rumors that the government would flee, and that Lincoln would resign.

Lincoln held firm, hastily started to reorganize his forces, and called for steady courage. Whitman cheered. He had found a new hero.

Walt's only weapon was his pen, and it was shortly after Bull Run that he wrote "Beat! Beat! Drums!" a call to arms that was closer to an editorial than a poem. But it reflected the new martial spirit of the awakened North. George, caught up in the same patriotic determination, re-enlisted for three years or the duration of the war, a recruit of the Fifty-first New York volunteers. This left Walt as the main support of his mother and Edward. Jeff was working and lived with his mother, but he had a wife and child to provide for. Jesse was unable even to help himself. Andrew was not only sickly but on the way to becoming an alcoholic, and had a family of his own.

Walt at the moment did not feel exactly like a man of iron himself. Aside from his depression over the war, his hopes of success for his new volume of *Leaves of Grass* had vanished. His enthusiastic publishers had gone bankrupt, and although there had been praise for the book as well as abuse and contempt, he was scarcely the widely acclaimed poet-prophet he had dreamed of being.

It was back to journalism for him—though back to new poems as well—with increasing visits to the hospital on Broadway and Pearl, where he had often called on sick stage drivers or firemen. He had become acquainted with the doctors on the staff and came and went freely, bringing presents to the invalids, sitting and talking and trying to cheer them up.

By the spring of 1862, several hundred soldiers took up bed space in the old hospital on Broadway. Walt began to visit them regularly on Sunday afternoons and evenings, and wrote articles for the newspapers about the hospital to try to raise funds for its upkeep. He had little enough money of his own to spare for charity; he was earning probably around six or seven dollars a week from newspaper work.

Mingled with all his other concerns was worry over George, who was in the thick of the fighting at the front. George had helped storm the Confederate forts at Roanoke and North Carolina, and had been made a second lieutenant. After the second battle of Bull Run, he was promoted to first lieutenant. During a lull in fighting, in September, he wrote home: ". . . I can imagine just what you are all doing at home and ile bet now, that Mother is making pies . . . Walt is upstairs writing, Jeff is down town at the office, Jess is pealing Potatoes for dinner, and Edward has gone down for a scuttle of coal."

In December, George was camped near Fredericksburg. On December 13th, a fierce battle took place there, and Whitman and his family read the newspapers with apprehension, scanning the first lists of the killed or wounded. On December 16th, the *Herald* published what was supposed to be a complete list of the casualties among the Fifty-first New York Volunteers. Among the names was that of "First Lieutenant G. W. Whitmore, Company D." The initials were George's, and he was a first lieutenant with the Volunteers. There was no doubt in the Whitman family's mind that George was meant, but the paper did not say how serious his wounds were. At least, there was no name in the list of those killed that resembled George's. Still, each member of the family had visions of George suffering alone, perhaps dying. Mrs. Whitman, beside herself with anxiety, looked to Walt to reassure her.

He would have to go to Washington, Walt decided, make all the inquiries he could, and visit the army hospitals. But he would need money for fare and lodging. The family got fifty dollars together and Walt set out, the money bundled into a purse carried in his pocket. At Philadelphia, where he had to change trains to take yet another train to Washington, the depot was crowded with other travelers. In the crush and confusion, Whitman was not aware of the hand that reached into his pocket and withdrew the purse. Consequently he arrived in the capital without money for even the basic necessities, let alone enough to pay for rides to the nearly forty military hospitals in and around the city. He experienced two days of the greatest misery he had ever known, he wrote his mother, "walking day and night, unable to ride, trying to get information . . . trying to get access to big people" for information.

Walt was close to despair when he ran into a friend he had made during his stay in Boston. This was William D. O'Connor, a strikingly handsome, vigorous young Irishman who was now employed as a clerk in the Treasury Department. O'Connor, a loyal defender and admirer of Whitman and his poetry, immediately took out his wallet, gave Walt money, and offered to help him in his search.

Neither the incomplete lists in the Washington papers nor the rosters at the hospitals made any mention of George. Walt decided that perhaps his brother might still be with his regiment across the river from Fredericksburg. The battle had been a disastrous one for the Army of the Potomac, under General Burnside, because of Burnside's procrastination. The blue-clad men had fought desperately to storm the heights across the Rappahannock River in the face of Confederate entrenchments. Driven back, the survivors of George's regiment were reported to be camped at Falmouth, on the Union side of the river. Walt discovered that he could go there part of the way by government boat and then finish the journey on a military train.

It was an arduous trip of some twenty-four hours. When he reached the camp the scene there was not one to lift his spirits. Searching out the Fifty-first Volunteers, he had to pass a large brick mansion on the banks of the river which was being used as a hospital. Outdoors, at the foot of a tree, was a heap of amputated feet, legs, arms, hands, and fingers, enough to fill a one-horse cart. Several dead bodies lay in the vicinity, each covered with a brown woolen blanket. Beyond stretched a row of freshly dug graves, the names of the dead crudely printed on pieces of barrel staves or broken boards thrust into the earth. Nor were all the wounded within the main hospital. Many lay in the tents, sometimes on the bare ground, although the ground was frozen. The sight, and the sounds, tore at Whitman, and his fears for George increased.

He found his brother standing among the tents and huts of the Fifty-first, on active duty, looking completely unharmed. Walt hurried to him to embrace him and then saw the wound in his brother's cheek. He learned that a shell fragment had pierced the cheek, but that the wound was healing well.

As for George, he was surprised to find Walt there. He had tried to make sure that his name would not be on the wounded list and had imagined that his family knew nothing about his being hit.

Now that Walt was here, why not stay a few days? George asked. Walt could share George's tent, learn more about the camp, and rest.

The exhausted Whitman eagerly accepted the invitation, but first he arranged to have the good news sent home by messenger and telegraph.

For about eight days, the big, gray-haired man in civilian clothes wandered around the camp and even went out under a flag of truce to help in the burial of the dead lying on the battlefield. He forced himself to visit the grim brick hospital that was crowded with more wounded men than the staff could cope with. At the door of the operating rooms he heard the terrible sound of a surgeon's saw droning above other sounds. A number of the wounded or sick were Rebel soldiers, but Whitman's pity did not stop at the sight of a gray uniform. He handed out newspapers or whatever else he had to give, wrote letters for the dying, or sat and talked to any who craved companionship.

He was still at camp at Christmas, and on that day he walked out to a campground deserted by soldiers, but still littered with abandoned tools and the trappings of war. There under the warm sunlight lay a broken cart, a boot with the sole ripped off, a bloody cap, the bloated and fly-covered body of a dead horse. The landscape as far as he could see was lifeless except for the continuing passage of caravans of six-mule teams dragging wagons loaded with military supplies. There was not a tree in sight, every tree having been cut down for wood fires or for building huts. Even fence posts were gone. In spite of the distant blare of bugles, the glimpse of a large troop of cavalry passing by, the horses' manes shaking, sabers gleaming in the sun, Walt was struck by the terrible cost and waste of war. That and the valor and suffering of the soldiers on both sides cried out for expression.

He sat on a pine log, brooding, remembering how one morning at daybreak he had crept out of his tent to find three forms lying on stretchers, covered with blankets. He had lifted the blanket from one figure.

> Who are you elderly man so gaunt and grim, with well-
> gray'd hair, and flesh all sunken about the eyes?
> Who are you my dear comrade?
>
> Then to the second I step—and who are you my child and
> darling?
> Who are you sweet boy with cheeks yet blooming?
>
> Then to a third—a face nor child nor old, very calm, as of
> beautiful yellow-white ivory;
> Young man I think I know you—I think this face is the
> face of the Christ himself,
> Dead and divine brother of all, and here again he lies.

It did no good to sit on a log and think of the bitterness of war, or of the dead. There were boys still living, here in the brick hospital and in the hospitals in Brooklyn, Manhattan, Washington—everywhere—to whom even an apple or a kindly word could make the difference between despair and hope. Both doctors and nurses were in short supply. He could not be a doctor, except of the spirit, but he could wash and cleanse the festering wounds, lift a moistened pad to parched mouths or hold a fever-shaken young man in the curve of his own strong arm. He had already done it here, had already made a place for himself with common soldier and officer alike.

He would do more, be both poet and wound dresser. Walking back toward the camp, he knew that he had found a new commitment and that by his search for a missing brother he had found a hundred thousand new brothers.

Walt Whitman had enlisted not just for three years or ten but for as long as it took and as long as his strength would last.

6

Flash of the Naked Sword

A train moved slowly toward the capital from the camp at Falmouth, the small locomotive straining at the string of cars behind it. On platform cars, ordinarily used for hauling inanimate cargo, sat or lay wounded soldiers. Traveling with them was Whitman—or "Walt," as the soldiers generally called him. At the landing where a steamer waited to take the men up the Potomac, Walt went among the stretchers, talking, taking messages, awkwardly trying to adjust a slipped bandage, bringing a needed dipper of water, almost forgetting to drink or eat, himself. He was in charge of this group and was determined to get every man to the Washington hospitals alive. But he could not perform miracles; one "poor fellow" died.

After seeing the living safely into the various hospitals, Walt went to see William O'Connor, his good friend of Boston days. He asked the O'Connors to help him find an inexpensive room, since he planned to stay in the city for a week or two in order to visit soldiers from Brooklyn.

The two could find nothing adequate for what Walt could afford, so they returned to the house where the O'Connors rented rooms on the third floor. The landlord agreed to rent a small bedroom on the second floor to Walt. Mrs. O'Connor, who had taken an instant liking to the poet, urged him to eat his meals with them without charge. Whitman accepted, believing that the arrangement would be only temporary. A few days later he ran into Charles Eldridge, one of the partners in the publishing firm that had had such high hopes for the third edition of *Leaves of Grass*. Maybe, said Eldridge, he could arrange some government employment for Whitman; Eldridge himself was assistant to the Army Paymaster. Eldridge succeeded in obtaining for Walt two to three hours a day of work in the Paymaster's office. Although the job paid little, it covered his expenses and left him many precious hours to visit the soldiers in the hospitals. So important to him were these visits, and so much did he feel needed by the soldiers, that he postponed his plans to return home, a postponement that went on for years.

At the beginning of his service to the wounded in the new year of 1863, he wrote to Jeff's wife, Martha, "I can be satisfied and happy henceforward if I can get one meal a day, and know that mother and all are in good health . . . How your heart would ache to go through the rows of wounded young men, as I did —and stopt to speak a comforting word to them."

Whitman did more than speak. He brought food, especially little delicacies that the men asked for. He wrote letters. He walked into the wards where smallpox and other contagious diseases threatened any visitor. He watched over individual cases that especially worried him and summoned the doctor to those who needed immediate attention. The soldiers began to wait for the visits of the "old man" with his sticks of horehound candy, his bits of tobacco, knickknacks, and compassionate concern.

Walt wrote down his impressions, leaving a picture of himself and of the patients in the wards. "The American soldier," he said, "is full of affection and the yearning for affection. And it comes wonderfully grateful to him to have this yearning gratified when he is laid up with painful wounds or illness, far away from home, among strangers. Many will think this merely senti-mentalism, but I know it is the most solid of facts. I believe that even the moving around among the men, or through the ward, of a hearty, healthy, clean, strong, generous-souled person, man or woman, full of humanity and love, sending out invisible, constant currents thereof, does immense good to the sick and wounded."

There is no doubt that Walt was the kind of person he de-scribed. He was "generous-souled." He was, at age forty-three, still healthy, almost fanatically clean, face, body, and hands scrubbed until they seemed to shine. Above all, he had a mag-netism that drew persons to him, a quality called *charisma*.

Although he belonged to no church, he had always been stirred by magnificent passages in the Bible, and he worshiped God, man, and nature in his own way. Among the many soldiers he took a special interest in was a dying young New Yorker, Oscar Wilber, who told Walt that his only consolation was his belief in God. "He asked me to read him a chapter of the New Testa-ment," Walt recorded. Whitman read the chapters describing the last hours of Christ and the crucifixion. "I read very slowly, for Oscar was feeble. It pleased him very much, yet the tears were in his eyes. He asked me if I enjoyed religion. I said, 'Perhaps not, my dear, in the way you mean, and yet maybe it is the same thing.' He behaved very manly and affectionate. The kiss I gave him as I was about leaving, he returned fourfold."

Young John Burroughs, who was to become famous as a writer and naturalist and who met Walt in these years, had this to say:

> I have been much with Walt . . . . The more I see and talk with him, the greater he becomes to me. He is as vast as the earth, and as loving and noble. He is much hand-somer than his picture represents him. . . . He does not

talk readily, but his conversation is very rich and suggestive. He regards Emerson as one of the great, eternal men. . . .

I am convinced that Walt is as great as Emerson, though after a different type. Walt has all types of men in him, there is not one left out.

The more Burroughs saw of Walt the more he liked him: ". . . so kind, sympathetic, charitable, humane, tolerant a man I did not suppose possible. He loves everything and everybody."

Burroughs, destined to become one of Whitman's greatest friends, recorded this in a matter-of-fact fashion. This was the way Walt was.

It was as he had been and would continue to be, not only toward friends and acquaintances, but toward the bickering members of his own family who often tried even his broad patience. His sister Hannah, a neurotic married to an equally neurotic husband, never ceased to complain about her lot, but Walt thought of her as "the fairest and most delicate of human blossoms." His mother, faithful housekeeper though she was, was not perhaps the radiant saint Walt described in his poems. Nor did she truly understand what his *Leaves of Grass,* his life work, was about.

"Who of my family has gone along with me?" Walt once said. "Not one of them. They have always missed my intentions. Take my darling dear mother . . . she had great faith in me—felt sure I would accomplish wonderful things: but *Leaves of Grass?* . . . She would shake her head. God bless her!" As for George, "It may be said that I love him—he loving me, too, in a certain way," but as far as George's understanding Walt's poems, they were far beyond him.

The family did understand Walt's labors in the army hospitals, for Jeff began enclosing small amounts of money in his letters, and tried to collect additional money from his fellow employees at the Brooklyn Water Works. Emerson and others in Concord also sent contributions, in answer to Whitman's solicitations. Even so, Whitman needed more money for his hospital work and began trying to find a higher paying job with the government. Emerson and other prominent men gave him letters of recommendation, and armed with these, Whitman began a career of office hunting that was to last two years. In the meantime, he had to struggle along as best he could, and again dreamed of setting out on a lecture tour, this time to raise money for soldiers' care.

He wrote faithfully to his mother about his labors for the sick and wounded and in April told her how large and well he was, weighing two hundred pounds and looking, he said, "like a great wild buffalo, with much hair." He was not quite as well as he claimed. The hospital visits from noon to four o'clock and then again from six in the evening until nine, seven hours of strain, pity, and often horror of the kind that made other visitors faint, were exhausting. In addition there was all his other work; his notebooks in which he recorded his impressions of the time, his job in the Paymaster's office, and his work on a new volume of poems. There was certainly very little time for the kind of activity he had described in "Song of Myself": "I loafe and invite my soul, I lean and loafe at my ease observing a spear of summer grass." Now he observed suffering and death. Many soldiers perished from the ignorant medical practices of the day, doctors having no understanding of the need for sterilizing instruments and dressings, so that even minor wounds could fester into fatal ones. Blood poisoning, gangrene, secondary infections, pneumonia, and dysentery killed thousands of men even in the best hospitals. In the worst hospitals, conditions were often so filthy or chaotic that to be sent to them was tantamount to a sentence of death.

Outside the hospital, too, there were constant reminders of the war. In summer heat or rain, trains of huge four-horse wagons used as ambulances rumbled from the Potomac wharves on their way to various hospitals. Everywhere around the city were soldiers and more soldiers, many carrying canes or using crutches. Whitman mingled with them, talking, listening. No history, no book, no poem, he thought, could ever give a full picture of their heroism. In his prose work, *Specimen Days,* he wrote, "Who [can] know the conflict, hand-to-hand—the many conflicts in the dark, those shadowy-tangled, flashing—moonbeamed woods—the writhing groups and squads—the cries, the din, the cracking guns and pistols—the distant cannon . . . the strong shout, *Charge, men, charge*—the flash of the naked sword, and rolling flame and smoke?"

Could President Lincoln know or even imagine? Certainly there was a terrible sadness in his face; Whitman could study it frequently, for his lodgings were on the street where Lincoln passed every day. To escape the crushing summer and fall heat, Lincoln spent his nights at the Soldiers' Home three miles north of the city.

"He always has a company of twenty-five or thirty cavalry, with sabers drawn and held upright over their shoulders. They say this guard was against his personal wish . . . Mr. Lincoln on the saddle generally rides a good-sized, easy-going gray horse, is dressed in plain black, somewhat rusty and dusty, wears a black stiff hat, and looks about as ordinary in attire, etc., as the commonest man." But the face of the President was not common. "I see very plainly ABRAHAM LINCOLN's dark brown face, with the deep-cut lines, the eyes, always to me with a deep latent sadness in the expression. We have got so that we exchange bows and very cordial ones."

Earlier in the summer, Lincoln, on a pleasure ride with his

wife, had passed very close to where Whitman was standing on the street. "I saw the President in the face fully, as they were moving slowly, and his look, though abstracted, happen'd to be directed steadily in my eye. He bow'd and smiled, but far beneath his smile I noticed well the expression I have alluded to. None of the artists or pictures has caught the deep, though subtle and indirect expression of this man's face. There is something else there."

From this it is clear that Lincoln recognized Whitman. He was already familiar with *Leaves of Grass* and undoubtedly knew, too, of Whitman's work with the wounded. It is said that a friend once pointed out the poet to Lincoln and the President remarked, "Well, he looks like a *man*."

There was no escape from the heat for Whitman. His small attic bedroom was often suffocating, as were the hospital wards, especially those that were housed in nothing much better than improvised sheds. There he sat by sweating men, trying vainly to cool them and himself with a cardboard fan. In the blazing streets, he carried an umbrella to shelter his head, for he was beginning to experience strange moments of dizziness. Doctors had warned him to cut down on his strenuous activities, but this he found hard to do. Although he was depressed at times by the "distress" in his head, he tried to make light of it. His health, of which he was vain, had never failed him yet. Still, there was a nagging worry in his mind.

The constant exposure to the casualties of the war contributed to his moments of depression. To his mother he wrote in September, 1863, "Mother, one's heart grows sick of war, after all, when you see what it really is: every once in a while I feel so horrified and disgusted—it seems to me like a great slaughterhouse and the men mutually butchering each other." His horror and pity deepened at last to the point that he cried out in a later letter to her about the agony he saw every day, "I get almost frightened at the world."

This is an unfamiliar, desperate, and pathetic note in the voice of the poet who had set out to celebrate the world, especially America, and who had chosen to radiate cheer in the bloody, groaning hospital wards. He still managed to be outwardly cheerful, and went from hospital to hospital, consciously cutting a fine figure in his broad, light-colored hat, wine-colored suit, a tie flowing down over frilled, white shirts his mother made especially for him. But underneath there was a growing realization that neither democracy nor brotherhood was to be won merely for the singing. The ground on which they would grow —for he still believed in their ultimate existence—was a dark and bloody one.

So, although he shrank from the carnage, he was still committed to hope and to the Union cause, as he was still committed to the poems he had poured out of himself at the beginning of the war. These, entitled *Drum-Taps,* were in his family's keeping in Brooklyn, unpublished because he could find no one to publish them. It was hard to know why, for into them he had put all his patriotism, optimism, and love for the nation. There was nothing in them to shock those delicate ears and minds that had reacted to earlier poems.

In late October, 1863, Walt found another person he would grow to love. This was John Burroughs, then only twenty-six, an ex-schoolteacher who still had no idea that he was eventually to become a famous naturalist. A shy, dark-eyed and dark-haired young man, Burroughs had read *Leaves of Grass* and everything else he could by Whitman, and had made Walt a hero even before their first meeting, which took place at an army supply store run by a friend of Burroughs. Although they liked each other at once, it was not until they met accidentally on a footpath later, Walt on his way to an army hospital, his haversack and pockets stuffed with gifts for the soldiers, that the two had a chance to find out how much they had in common. Burroughs accompanied Walt to the hospital and saw at first hand not only the grisly sights that made him shudder but Walt's selfless devotion to the maimed, the despondent, and the dying. Just to be in Walt's company was a pleasure to Burroughs, compensation during his early weeks in Washington when he was looking for work, almost penniless, and lonely for his wife. He slept on a cot in his friend's store.

After they met, Walt and Burroughs took many walks together, and began calling each other "Jack" and "Walt." Burroughs wrote of Walt in his notebooks that there was something "indescribable in his look, in his eye, as that in the mother of many children."

To Walt, Jack Burroughs offered the kind of comradeship he had so often written about and yearned for, a comradeship that was to continue and ripen in the years ahead.

In November, during a trip home to Brooklyn, Walt wrote to Charles Eldridge: "I feel to devote myself more to the work of my life, which is making poems. I must bring out Drum Taps. I *must* be continually bringing out poems—now is the hey day. I shall range along the high plateau of my life and capacity for a few years now, and then swiftly descend. . . ."

He was still not feeling well and had come home to rest a bit as much as to see the family for whom he had been lonesome. A second child had been born to Jeff and Martha in June, and Whitman could enjoy himself, cradling the infant. Otherwise, the household was rather grim, Andrew spending most of his time at home now, weak from swiftly spreading tuberculosis of the throat, and Jesse so irrational that Jeff kept nagging Mrs. Whitman to have him committed to an asylum. Money was as hard to come by as ever. Whitman, in fact, had not had money for his train fare from Washington. His good friend O'Connor had managed to get him a government pass through Lincoln's secretary, John Hay. Going to pick up the pass at the President's house, Whitman had again seen Lincoln close at hand as Lincoln stood talking to another caller. Walt found Lincoln's face and manner "inexpressibly sweet." He confided in his notebook, "I love the President personally."

Walt left Brooklyn for Washington on December 1st. Two days after his arrival in the capital, Jeff sent a telegram saying that Andrew was dead; Walt was remorseful that he had not stayed home a few more days to be there when the end came.

Later in the month there was more depressing news from Jeff. Jesse, Jeff wrote, was practically a maniac and was, Jeff was certain, shortening their mother's life. "He calls her everything—and even swears he will keel her over."

In response to a questioning letter from Walt, Mrs. Whitman wrote, admitting that "Jesse is a very great trouble to me to be sure and dont apprecete what i doo for him but he is no more deranged than he has been for the last 3 years i think it would be very bad for him to be put in the lunatic assilyim . . . i think Walt what a poor unfortunate creature he has been . . . as long as i can get any thing for him to eat i would rather work and take [care] of him that is as long as i see no danger of harm."

It was not a cheerful Christmas. Even Walt's lodgings were depressing, at least in the eyes of a visitor who called on him. The man was John T. Trowbridge, who had come from Boston to get material for a biography of Salmon Chase, Lincoln's Secretary of the Treasury. Trowbridge interviewed Chase in his fine mansion on Pennsylvania Avenue and then learned to his surprise, through O'Connor, that Whitman, whose poetry Trowbridge admired, lived diagonally opposite Chase in a small garret room.

With O'Connor, Trowbridge called on the poet. He recorded his dismay: "In the old tenement opposite, in a bare and desolate back room, up three flights of stairs, quite alone, lived the poet. Walt led the way up those dreary stairs, partly in darkness, found the keyhold of a door which he unlocked and opened, scratched a match, and welcomed us to his garret." [There was scarcely any more furniture] "than a bed, a cheap pine table, and a little sheet-iron stove in which there was no fire. Walt, clearing a chair or two of their litter of newspapers, invited us to sit down and stop awhile, with as simple and sweet hospitality as if he had been offering us the luxuries of the great mansion across the square."

Two days later, Trowbridge called again in the morning. Walt was fixing his breakfast on the little stove. Using his jackknife, he sliced some bread, and while Trowbridge toasted it for him over the stove, made tea. He dipped sugar out of a brown paper bag and used a scrap of the same kind of paper for a butter plate. When he was through eating, he burned his butter plate, then opened a trunk and took out the manuscript of *Drum-Taps*. He read the poems aloud, "unaffectedly, with force and feeling, and in a voice of rich but not resonant tones."

Trowbridge left, determined to try to help Whitman find the government post he had been seeking. He took Emerson's letter of recommendation with him and called at Salmon Chase's mansion. There he presented the letter, adding his own personal recommendation. Chase was impressed that Whitman had been recommended by so distinguished a man as Emerson, but murmured that he had heard Whitman had written a notorious and objectionable book, so he could do nothing. He did do something, however; he appropriated the Emerson letter for his own collection, much to Trowbridge's shock and dismay.

In February, 1864, Walt made a trip to the battlefront at Culpepper, Virginia. Mingling with the soldiers, watching them march through deep mud, burdened with overcoats, knapsacks, guns, and blankets, but still able to laugh and sing, he was impressed again by "the majesty and reality of the American people *en masse*. It fell upon me like a great awe." As for the Virginia landscape, dilapidated, fenceless, and war-scarred though it was, Whitman was filled with admiration for the richness of the soil, the breadth of the scenery with distant mountains everywhere. The skies and atmosphere he found "most luscious . . . The sun rejoices in his strength, dazzling and burning, and yet, to me, never unpleasantly weakening."

Nevertheless, he did not have his usual sense of robust, physical well-being. The strain of his vigils at the hospitals and the gathering maladies within his own body were making themselves felt, although not yet in an alarming way. Back in Washington, he continued his rounds from one hospital to another. Sometimes the humblest of gifts seemed to be the most welcome. "The men like to have a pencil, and something to write in. I have given them cheap pocket diaries, and almanacs for 1864, interleaved with blank paper. For reading I generally have some old pictorial magazines or story papers—they are always acceptable. Also the morning or evening papers of the day."

In the newspapers the soldiers could read of the progress of the war. In spite of General Lee's defeat at the battle of Gettysburg, when he had attempted to invade the North the year before, his army had managed to retreat successfully to Virginia. There, apparently invincible, the Rebel soldiers barred the roads along which Union armies would have to march if they tried to drive into the Confederacy's eastern stronghold.

The Army of the Potomac was still so ineffective that some Congressmen were willing to call it quits and recognize Jefferson Davis' Confederacy. Sick though Walt was of war, he believed that it must continue, and was tempted to enlist in the ranks. Still, perhaps he was more valuable where he was, he reflected. Nor was he a stalwart eighteen-year-old, like so many of the soldiers—some were even younger. At age forty-five, it might not be easy to wade through mud, or tramp along through dust and heat.

George, after a thirty-day furlough, had re-enlisted. In April, Burnside's army trooped through Washington. Walt, certain that George would be among them, stood watching the 30,000 men march by for three hours, searching for a glimpse of his brother. Then, suddenly, he saw him, and strode over to fall into step beside him. Ahead was the President in the reviewing stand. George became so excited at seeing Walt that he marched past Lincoln and the other dignitaries, completely forgetting to salute.

In June, the Washington heat intensified once more. Around the middle of the month, soldiers at Carver Hospital were astonished and delighted to see their friend Walt Whitman supervising the distribution of a great quantity of ice cream which he had purchased for them. The cool, delicious gift was one that the soldiers would remember.

Walt had still not procured the office job he sought, and he was beginning to find the strain of the war overwhelming. The sight of ambulances rolling on and on from the Potomac docks, the fevers and wounds, the tension of wondering whether General Ulysses Grant would succeed in his drive to Richmond, tightened his nerves so that at times he felt faint. He had developed an infection in his throat, too, that added to his discomfort and anxiety. In the meantime, no one seemed to want to publish either his *Drum-Taps* or his prose writings about the war. He wrote to his mother that he planned to come home as soon as the outcome of Grant's campaign was known. He was worried, too, about George, who had taken part in some of the fiercest battles of the war at the Rapidan River and was now fighting in the Virginia wilderness. He was waiting and hoping for news from George.

Toward the end of June, Walt felt too ill to "hang on" in Washington any longer. Homesick and exhausted, he made his way to Brooklyn. There he suffered a kind of general collapse and was not even able to leave the house until July 8th.

By September he felt much better and went two or three times a week to visit the soldiers in the Brooklyn hospitals. He also managed to pursue some of his old, beloved activities—sailing on the bay, visiting New York, talking with his former cronies, attending political meetings there or in Brooklyn with their exciting fireworks, cannon, clusters of gas lights, torches and banners. Yet, he did not feel quite as hearty as he had before his sickness. And in October, he and the family had fresh worries about George. Since a battle at the end of September, no word had been heard from him, and Walt was certain that if he was still alive he was a prisoner.

Then, there was the problem of Jesse's increasing violence. It was Walt who had to carry out the final decision as to what was to be done. On December 5th, grim and heartsick, Walt committed his brother to the Kings County Lunatic Asylum.

The day after Christmas, George's trunk arrived by express, having been sent by one of his regiment. It stood in the house several hours before anyone had the heart to open it.

"There were many things reminded us of him. Papers, memoranda, books, nick-nacks, a revolver, a small diary, roll of his company, a case of photographs of his comrades (several of them I knew as killed in battle) . . . Mother looked everything over, laid out the shirts to be washed . . . It made us feel pretty solemn."

But there was a bright spot in this troubled December. O'Connor, who with other friends had kept trying to find a government post for Whitman, wrote that there were good prospects for a job for Walt in the Interior Department and instructed him to send in his application.

Walt did as he was told, and on January 12th of the new year, the Assistant Secretary of the Department wrote that upon reporting to the Department and passing an examination he would be appointed to a clerkship at twelve hundred dollars a year— Walt's first salaried job since his editorship of the Brooklyn *Times* eight years before.

The examination was apparently only a formality, so when Walt set out for Washington it was with confidence that the job was his. Except for Jesse, whom he visited at the asylum before he left, things looked much brighter. He had finally heard from George, who had written from the Confederate Military Prison at Danville, Virginia. George said that he was feeling fine and that his family should not worry. Walt was determined to try to get his brother released, hopefully through an exchange of prisoners from both sides.

On the train, feeling physically and spiritually refreshed, Walt looked forward to his good friends in Washington, his visits to the soldiers, and the eventual end of the war. The tide had turned and a Union victory was only a matter of time. Perhaps, too, he could at last publish *Drum-Taps*.

> A march in the ranks, hard-prest, and the road unknown,
> A route through a heavy wood with muffled steps in the
>   darkness . . .

But, it seemed, the darkness was lifting.

7

I Give You My Sprig of Lilac

Never before had there been such a mass of people inside the White House and out as on the evening of Lincoln's second inauguration, March, 1865. Victory for the North was in the air, and people poured in from everywhere to shake Lincoln's hand at the public reception he held. Whitman surged forward with the rest, eager to have still another look at the man he had come to revere as the very symbol of democracy. There Lincoln stood, dressed in black as usual, wearing white kid gloves and a claw-hammer coat, dutifully shaking hands but looking as if he would have preferred to be almost anywhere else.

Although Whitman enjoyed the bedlam, the fine music of the Marine band, and the sight of rough country people all around, he was well aware of the rumors that had been circulating that there were plans to abduct or assassinate the President. The weather had a strange, dramatic quality that day—beginning in fierce thunder and lightning, then clearing so that after the inauguration ceremony, Whitman remembered later, "as the President came out on the Capitol portico, a curious little white cloud, the only one in that part of the sky, appeared like a hovering bird, right over him."

In the days following, the weather was continuously beautiful. This and news from Walt's mother that George had arrived safely home from military prison made Walt feel especially heartened. He had appealed for his brother's release by a letter to General Grant, and Grant had intervened. Eager to see George, Walt arranged for a two weeks' leave from his clerkship and hurried home.

Aside from being thinner and bothered by rheumatism, George looked better than Walt had expected. He, himself, was feeling fine and looking forward to news of the end of the war.

Lilacs were beginning to bloom in both Brooklyn and in southern cities on the Palm Sunday when the war came to a formal end. At the village of Appomattox, in southern Virginia, two men confronted each other. Tall, handsome, aristocratic General Robert E. Lee, a sword still belted to his waist, faced the officer who had done most to crush the armies of the South. General Ulysses S. Grant, rather short, still in mudspattered boots and rumpled blue coat, swordless, tried to soften the occasion for the other man, making small talk before getting to the main business of the meeting—the total surrender of the Confederate army.

Like other Northerners Whitman was exultant. Yet, joy was streaked through by sorrow for all the brave men who had perished. "The dead in this war," Whitman mourned, "—there they lie, strewing the fields and woods and valleys and battlefields . . . *our* dead—or South or North, ours all (all, all, all, finally dear to me)—the infinite dead (the land entire saturated, perfumed with their impalpable ashes' exhalation in Nature's chemistry distilled, and shall be so forever, in every future grain of wheat and ear of corn, and every flower that grows . . .)"

There were still thousands of living soldiers, however, to care for, and Whitman's long role of wound-dresser was not yet ended.

Bearing the bandages, water and sponge,
Straight and swift to my wounded I go . . .

I am faithful, I do not give out,
The fractured thigh, the knee, the wound in the abdomen,
These and more I dress with impassive hand, (yet deep in
my breast a fire, a burning flame.)

For the moment he was still in Brooklyn with problems of his own, particularly the need of trying to push through publication of *Drum-Taps*. Since no one else would print it, he resolved to do it himself. Printers urged him to wait until the cost of paper and printing went down from inflated war levels. Wait. It seemed to him that he had been doing that far too long, and he decided to go ahead. In order to begin the project, he asked for an extra week's leave from his Washington post, and he was still at home with his family on April 15th, Good Friday, when the news of Lincoln's assassination came. The night before, the newspapers reported, the President had been shot at Ford's Theatre while he sat and watched a stage performance. The murderer, John Wilkes Booth, had escaped.

Whitman and his family were stunned. Walt later wrote of the family's reaction: "Mother prepared breakfast—and other meals afterward—as usual; but not a mouthful was eaten all day by either of us. We each drank half a cup of coffee; that was all. Little was said. We got every newspaper morning and evening, and the frequent extras of that period, and passed them silently to each other."

In the afternoon, rain falling steadily from a dark sky, Walt boarded the ferry and crossed the river to Manhattan. Almost every store was closed. The fronts of buildings were draped with black. A great quietness, scarcely broken by the rumble of an occasional cart or Broadway stagecoach, lay over everything, even the few people in the streets. In almost every face Whitman saw a strange mixture of horror, fury, pity and consternation. Even the sky seemed to reflect the somberness with long, broad black clouds undulating like serpents in every direction. By six o'clock, dense throngs collected near the bulletin boards in front of the newspaper buildings. Whatever the others felt—and many muttered of revenge, believing that the murder was a plot of the Confederacy—Whitman was stricken with a sense of deep personal loss. He remembered the glorious evening star that had seemed to throb in the west after Lincoln's inauguration. Never, so long as he could remember, had Venus been so large and clear. It had seemed to portend some superb splendor.

Instead, in this month of blossom and renewal, the preserver of the Union, the author of the Emancipation Proclamation which had declared that Negro slaves should be forever free, lay as dead as any dead soldier on the battlefield. Riding homeward again over the East River waters he knew so well, Whitman sought for lines and symbols that could somehow memorialize the tragedy of the event.

Back in Washington by the following Monday, he was again confronted by signs of mourning—quiet streets and black-draped buildings—although underneath the seeming inactivity there were hectic preparations for the President's funeral. On Tuesday, the President's body lay in state on a catafalque in the East Room. Whitman did not join the procession tramping all day long past the bier. Having often seen the living Lincoln, he had no need to see him in death. He did, however, watch the long, solemn funeral procession the next day and heard the muffled drum beats, seeming echoes of the death march he had known as a boy in Brooklyn after the explosion aboard the *Fulton*. Following the funeral ceremonies in Washington, Lincoln's actual burial was to take place in his home state of Illinois. On Friday, the train bearing his body started off on the long journey.

Whitman swiftly wrote a poem to commemorate the occasion of the Washington service, "Hushed Be the Camps Today". Short, and not especially distinguished, it was only a practice piece, a preparation for the splendid elegy that was still only half-formed in his mind and heart, but which, when finished, would be one of his masterpieces:

When lilacs last in the dooryard bloom'd,
And the great star early droop'd in the western sky in the
      night,
I mourn'd, and yet shall mourn with ever-returning spring.

Ever-returning spring, trinity sure to me you bring,
Lilac blooming perennial and drooping star in the west,
And thought of him I love.

Coffin that passes through lanes and streets,
Through day and night with the great cloud darkening the
      land,
With the pomp of the inloop'd flags with the cities draped
      in black,
With the show of the States themselves as of crape-veil'd
      women standing,
With processions long and winding and the flambeaus of
      the night,
With the countless torches lit, with the silent sea of faces
      and the unbared heads,
With the waiting depot, the arriving coffin, and the sombre
      faces . . .

The dim-lit churches and the shuddering organs—where
    amid these you journey,
With the tolling tolling bells' perpetual clang,
Here, coffin that slowly passes,
I give you my sprig of lilac.

Into this long elegy Whitman wound a kind of musical spool
around the images of lilac, the coffin, the song of a solitary hermit thrush, pictures of Manhattan and America, fallen armies
and fields, and a carol of joy "to thee O death." Shining through
the whole is the image of the great star he had been so impressed
with following Lincoln's inauguration:

O western orb sailing the heaven,
Now I know what you must have meant a month since I
    walk'd,
As I walk'd in silence the transparent shadowy night,
As I saw you had something to tell as you bent to me night
    after night . . .

The solitary thrush, the "hermit withdrawn to himself, avoiding the settlements," becomes a symbol for Whitman's own song:

Song of the bleeding throat,
Death's outlet song of life, (for well dear brother I know,
If thou was not granted to sing thou would'st surely die.)

O how shall I warble myself for the dead one there I loved?
And how shall I deck my song for the large sweet soul
    that has gone?

Finally, the bird's voice and his own join in a duet to the mystic idea of death, accepting and even praising death as in his earlier poem, "Out of the Cradle Endlessly Rocking." Now, he writes:

Come lovely and soothing death,
Undulate around the world, serenely arriving, arriving,
In the day, in the night, to all, to each,
Sooner or later delicate death.

Dark mother always gliding near with soft feet,
Have none chanted for thee a chant of fullest welcome?
Then I chant it for thee, I glorify thee above all,
I bring thee a song that when thou must indeed come,
    come unfalteringly.

From me to thee glad serenades,
Dances for thee I propose saluting thee, adornments and
    feastings for thee,
And the sights of the open landscape and the high-spread
    sky are fitting,
And life and the fields, and the huge and thoughtful night.

At the end, Whitman ties together the three main images of the star, the bird, and the springtime motif of the lilac:

Yet each to keep and all, retrievements out of the night,
The song, the wondrous chant of the gray-brown bird,
And the tallying chant, the echo arous'd in my soul,

With the lustrous and drooping star with the countenance
    full of woe,
With the holders holding my hand nearing the call of the
    bird,
Comrades mine and I in the midst, and their memory ever
    to keep, for the dead I loved so well,
For the sweetest, wisest soul of all my days and lands—
    and this for his dear sake,
Lilac and star and bird twined with the chant of my soul,
There in the fragrant pines and the cedars dusk and dim.

In this poem, Whitman reached a peak of expression, skillfully weaving the many fabrics on his poetic loom into an intricate but unified pattern.

There was a new resident in the White House, Vice President Andrew Johnson who had been sworn in as the Chief Executive. "Very plain and substantial," Whitman described him. "It seemed wonderful that just that plain middling-sized ordinary man, dressed in black, without the least badge or ornament, should be the master of all these myriads of soldiers. . . ." For the returning Union armies had been pouring into Washington, legions from Vicksburg, from Richmond, from the Chattanooga and the Rapidan, from mountain, gulch, and prairie, gathering for the tremendous spectacle, the Grand Review. All day long on the twenty-third and the twenty-fourth of May, the men in blue marched down Pennsylvania Avenue, their ranks stretching as far as one could see, twenty and twenty-five abreast, flags streaming in the sunlit weather.

In this same month, Whitman brought out his book *Drum-Taps* in pamphlet form. It was not a collection of war poems only, although the emphasis was on those. In one of the poems, "Beat!

Beat! Drums!" he tries to show how the Civil War invaded all lives:

> Beat! beat! drums!—blow! bugles! blow!
> Through the windows—through doors—burst like a ruth-
> less force,
> Into the solemn church, and scatter the congregation,
> Into the school where the scholar is studying;
> Leave not the bridegroom quiet—no happiness must he
> have now with his bride,
> Nor the peaceful farmer any peace, ploughing his field or
> gathering his grain,
> So fierce you whirr and pound you drums—so shrill you
> bugles blow.

Against the backdrop of conflict and bloodshed, there were still the tranquillities of nature, as in "Bivouac on a Mountain Side":

> I see before me now a traveling army halting,
> Below a fertile valley spread, with barns and the orchards
> of summer,
> Behind, the terraced sides of a mountain, abrupt, in places
> rising high,
> Broken, with rocks, with clinging cedars, with tall shapes
> dingily seen,
> The numerous camp-fires scatter'd near and far, some away
> up on the mountain,
> The shadowy forms of men and horses, looming large-
> sized, flickering,
> And over all the sky—the sky! far, far out of reach, studded,
> breaking out, the eternal stars.

As in earlier poems of praise and hope, Whitman's exuberant affirmation of life, in nature or in cities, burst forth in "Give Me the Splendid Silent Sun." The lines ring with energy and acceptance of the world, regardless of the "war-strife":

> Give me the splendid silent sun with all his beams full-
> dazzling,
> Give me juicy autumnal fruit ripe and red from the orchard,
> Give me a field where the unmow'd grass grows,
> Give me an arbor, give me the trellis'd grape,
> Give me fresh corn and wheat, give me serene-moving ani-
> mals teaching content,
> Give me nights perfectly quiet as on high plateaus west of
> the Mississippi, and I looking up at the stars,
> Give me odorous at sunrise a garden of beautiful flowers
> where I can walk undisturb'd,
> Give me for marriage a sweet-breath'd woman of whom I
> should never tire,
> Give me a perfect child, give me away aside from the noise
> of the world a rural domestic life,
> Give me to warble spontaneous songs recluse by myself,
> for my own ears only,
> Give me solitude, give me Nature, give me again O Nature
> your primal sanities!

The repetition of "Give" for eleven lines is a deliberate contrast to the lines in section "2" that repeat "Keep" as the beginning words:

> Keep your splendid silent sun,
> Keep your woods O Nature, and the quiet places by the
> woods . . .

The poem switches back to "Give me . . ." again: ". . . faces and streets . . . Broadway . . . Manhattan . . The life of the theatre, bar-room, huge hotel . . . Manhattan faces and eyes forever for me." What he is saying is that although he craves nature's "primal sanities" his final allegiance is to the human scene, to "People, endless, streaming with strong voices, passions, pageants. . . ."

Whitman considered *Drum-Taps* superior to *Leaves of Grass*, more nearly perfect as a work of art. Because it was so bound up with the anguish of wounded and suffering young men, "The book is therefore unprecedently sad . . . but it also has the blast of the trumpet, and the drum pounds and shirrs in it, and then an undertone of sweetest comradeship and human love. . . ." But he wrote to O'Connor, "Still, Leaves of Grass is dear to me, always dear to me, as my first born . . ."

After writing "When Lilacs Last in the Dooryard Bloomed," Walt wanted to include it, and some other poems, in his *Drum-Taps* volume, so he recalled the original pamphlet and reissued it at the end of the year with the additional poems bound in.

Unfortunately, his reputation as a writer of "indecent" poetry had become so well established that many would not now read anything written by Whitman even though in some of the *Drum-Taps* poems the language was closer to that of the more conventional poetry of the day. Not that Whitman, the stubborn independent, was pandering to popular taste. Certainly he was not in the elegy to Lincoln. The "thee's" and "thou's" were deliberately used, to lift the poem into a lofty, religious sphere, as if it were a hymn. As for the inverted first line, how much it would have lost in music if he had written, "When lilacs bloomed in the dooryard last spring . . ."

But there was one poem in the volume which should have pleased even the most enthusiastic admirers of the kind of verse being written by the popular Longfellow. This was the completely un-Whitmanesque "O Captain! My Captain!" Strapped into regular, sing-song rhyme, it is one of the weakest poems he ever wrote. Yet this actually maudlin poem has been the most quoted, memorized, and admired by thousands of undiscriminating readers over the years. Popular anthologies and many school teachers have forced it on the public and on children to such an extent that even today Whitman is best known for this piece of melodramatic doggerel.

One of the first reviews of *Drum-Taps* was written by the same William Dean Howells who had been so delighted to meet Whitman and have Walt's great hand reach out to grasp his. The genteel Howells still liked Whitman the man, but could not say much for his poetry, although he found that the new poems were somewhat less crude than those in *Leaves of Grass*. Still, he thought Whitman's methods were wrong and that he could not be called a true poet.

Young Henry James, only at the beginning of his career as a successful novelist, found that it was a melancholy chore to read *Drum-Taps* and an equally melancholy chore to review it. Whitman could bear up under this kind of comment—he was pretty well accustomed to abuse by now—but he was stung deeply by the innuendo in James's comments about his work among sick soldiers.

"Like hundreds of other good patriots during the last four years," James wrote in his review, "Mr. Walt Whitman has imagined that a certain amount of violent sympathy with the great deeds and sufferings of our soldiers, and of admiration for our national energy, together with a ready command of picturesque language, are sufficient inspiration for a poet." James dismissed Whitman's selfless devotion in the hospital wards as mere "violent sympathy" and implied that Whitman had exploited those experiences to gain a literary reputation. Yet even as James wrote, Whitman was continuing to make his faithful visits to the hospitals, trying to console the pathetic, lingering cases, many of which were incurable. By December, 1865, only one military hospital remained active, Harewood Hospital, about three miles from the Capitol. There Whitman trudged as usual with his presents and his love.

There were others in the world besides critics and carpers, however. There were great good friends to compensate Walt, and he spent happy days with the O'Connors and John Burroughs and his wife. Burroughs had found a position in the Treasury Department and had rented a sturdy red-brick house and an acre of ground on Capitol Hill. There Burroughs busily hoed his garden, watched over his chickens and turned his cow, Chloe, out to grass—keeping an eye out for Whitman's frequent arrivals for breakfast or dinner. Walt was almost always late, and Ursula Burroughs would find herself with a smoking griddle and boiling coffee, everything ready for the meal, but no Whitman. One after another the horse-drawn cars would go by without stopping. When it seemed that Walt would never come, or that the pancake batter would collapse from fatigue, the big poet would finally roll off a car and saunter to the door, so smiling and good-humored that it was impossible to be angry. After the meal, Walt and Jack took long rambles in the woods, Burroughs contributing his growing knowledge of flora and fauna to Whitman.

On May 11, 1865, Whitman was promoted up the second rung of the ladder in his clerk's job. This recognition of his ability and the increased salary were especially welcome as the burden of supporting his mother and his brother Edward had fallen largely on his shoulders. Jeff, especially, resented Ed, believing that he was an impossible burden for Mother Whitman and declaring that he would not contribute financially unless she put Ed away somewhere in a boarding home. Walt sympathized with his mother's desire to keep Ed beside her.

Four days after Walt's promotion, a new Secretary of the Interior, James Harlan, a former Senator from Iowa and a former Methodist minister, took office. One of Harlan's first steps was to issue a circular to the heads of the bureaus in the department, asking them to report on the loyalty of the employees under them and their moral character.

Whitman's *Leaves of Grass* came to Harlan's attention. Whitman was revising the Thayer and Eldridge text in preparation for a fourth edition, and he left his copy in his office desk. Someone snooped—either Harlan himself or an underling—and the new Secretary went over the volume with its penciled changes and additions with a sharp, suspicious and presumably shocked eye. Without warning Whitman received an official message, dated June 30th, that his services would be dispensed with after that date.

It was disastrous and humiliating news, and Whitman went at once to his faithful and fiery friend, William O'Connor. O'Connor responded with typical indignation. Bearing Harlan's letter in his hand, O'Connor rushed to the office of the Attorney General, J. Hubley Ashton, and demanded to know why such rank injustice had taken place. Impassioned and eloquent, O'Connor declared that such an ignominious dismissal from public service of the greatest poet America had produced was an offense against the honor and dignity of American letters and against humanity itself. Ashton agreed that the wrong was a serious one and promised to talk to Harlan.

Harlan was adamant. Not if President Johnson himself asked him to reinstate Whitman, would he do it. The only thing he would agree to, in response to Ashton's plea, was not to oppose Whitman's appointment to some other department. If some other office wanted him, all right, just so Harlan did not have to have this immoral writer in his department.

On July 1st, thanks to Ashton, Whitman was given a new post in the Attorney General's Department.

The news of Whitman's dismissal was well-publicized in the newspapers, and old enemies among journalists enjoyed themselves describing the incident and Whitman's reputation for having allegedly written indecent poetry. The editor of the Brooklyn *Eagle* claimed that Whitman was "rather too much a child of nature" even for Emerson, and had written of "things no right-minded person is supposed ever to think of, and used language shocking to polite ears."

Nevertheless, Whitman's friends had carried the day. Secure again in his employment, Whitman could settle down and concentrate on the next edition of *Leaves of Grass*. O'Connor, however, still burned with anger over the whole affair and was indignant over the claims that Whitman's poetry was obscene. He decided to defend his friend to the world by means of a book of his own, and at the same time to defend the freedom of literature generally. He set to work with idealistic enthusiasm on the work, which he called *The Good Gray Poet*.

Early in January, 1866, O'Connor published his pamphlet Along with slashing attacks on those who wanted to censor literature to make it more acceptable to prigs, he created a portrait of Whitman that presented him not only as a genius but as a saint, almost a second Christ. Whitman's compassion and selflessness, O'Connor declared, was the strongest and truest he had ever known. Although he exaggerated Whitman's saintliness, he did make a strong and scholarly argument in defense of honesty and frankness in literature, pointing out that much of Shake-speare and the Bible would have to be deleted if the genteel censors had their way.

The book created a stir among literary circles. It did help to bring *Drum-Taps* some extra attention, but most of it was unfavorable.

"Time will remember him," O'Connor had declared of Whitman. Whitman had the same hope, and he clung to it in the face of continuing disappointment over the reception of his work. In the meantime, he had found a new friend among the laboring classes that had always attracted him. This was eighteen-year-old Peter Doyle, an Irish boy from Virginia who had fought for the South, been taken prisoner, and then transferred to Washington. After being paroled he became a conductor on a horse-drawn street car.

One stormy winter night, Walt boarded the car on his way home after a visit to the Burroughses.

"The storm was awful," Doyle remembered years later. "Walt had his blanket—it was thrown around his shoulders—he seemed like an old sea captain. He was the only passenger, it was a lonely night, so I thought I would go in and talk with him. Something in me made me do it and something in him drew me that way. . . . Anyway, I went into the car. We were familiar at once —I put my hand on his knee—we understood. He did not get out at the end of the trip—in fact went all the way back with me. . . . From that time on we were the biggest sort of friends."

A lonely night, said Peter Doyle. Apparently it was he who was lonely, enough to start talking to a stranger in spite of his basic shyness. Simple, poorly educated, but affectionate, he appealed to Whitman in the way that young soldiers, firemen, butcher boys, or other young men did. Whitman had been father and mother both to many a young soldier and now he treated young Doyle in the same way, calling him, as the friendship ripened, "dear son, my darling boy, my young and loving brother. . . ."

Pete went often to the Attorney General's office to visit Walt. Walt, in turn, often rode in Pete's horse-car. Frequently, at night, Walt accompanied him to the end of the line.

"Everybody knew him," Pete said. "He had a way of taking the measure of the drivers' hands—had calfskin gloves made for them every winter. . . . He saluted the men on the other cars as we passed—threw up his hand. They cried to him, 'Hullo, Walt!' and he would reply, 'Ah, there!' or something like. He was welcome always as the flowers in May. . . ."

The friendship between Whitman and Doyle was the longest and apparently the most intense relationship in Whitman's life. Whitman described Doyle as "a big rounded everyday workingman, full to the brim with the real substance of God." Although Whitman tended to find divinity in practically every human being, some quality in Peter Doyle made him respond with extra admiration.

Whenever Walt was away from the city, he wrote faithfully to his young friend, and Doyle answered. Walt wrote out his concern and devotion, worrying about Doyle's health, sending money when he thought it was needed—in the same way that he helped other young or sick workingmen in times of financial stress. At one time, when Whitman was visiting in Providence, he wrote to Doyle about the abundance of fresh fruit and flowers available there: "Pete, I could send you a bouquet every morning far better than I used to—of much choicer flowers. And how are you getting along, dearest comrade? . . . I am luxuriating on excellent grapes, I wish I could send you a basket."

Although Doyle was, for at least a dozen years, his chief friend and comrade, Whitman had many others, and he did not desert his earlier friends. Some of these were young workingmen whom both he and Doyle knew. In one of his letters to Doyle, Whitman asks Pete to "give my love to Johnny Lee, my dear darling boy. I love him truly—"

Not only did the physical robustness of young laborers and their simplicity appeal to Walt, but he greatly admired their mastery of their jobs, their skill with hammers, hooks, axes, reins. Especially, he enjoyed the common speech, and slang, used by most manual workers. Such slang, he thought, enlivened the American language, renewed and freshened it. He used slang expressions himself, even in his poetry.

At the time Whitman met Peter Doyle he still had dizzy spells, especially in the hot sun, but on the whole he was enjoying life. In August he took a leave from his job to apply himself to the fourth edition of *Leaves of Grass*—"that unkillable work," as he called it. He boarded with a Mrs. Abby Price and her daughter Helen.

"He seemed to call forth the best there was in those he met," Helen Price remembered. "He never appeared to me a conceited or egotistical man, though I have frequently heard him say himself that he was so." While he was boarding at the house and working on his new edition, she noticed one evening at dinner how "there seemed to be a peculiar brightness and elation about him, an almost irrepressible joyousness, which shone from his face and seemed to pervade his whole body."

In October, Walt was excited and pleased to learn that his work had received a very favorable review in one of England's outstanding publications. Then, in November, he received another promotion, to a permanent clerkship, with another boost in salary, to $1,600 a year. He increased the amount of money he sent home regularly to his mother. Nor had he forgotten his soldier friends. At Christmas, for those still in the hospital, he arranged a feast which included everything from turkey to mince pie.

After the first of the year, he received another small raise in salary and decided that he could afford to move from the grim, unheated room he had been renting. He found a more comfortable attic room in a boardinghouse. John Burroughs had brought out a fine review of *Drum-Taps,* and O'Connor managed to get a four column review of *Leaves of Grass* in *The New York Times.*

Things were looking up for Walt and his work, especially in England, with the possibility that *Leaves of Grass* might be published there. Jeff, too, was doing well, going to St. Louis to be the Superintendent of the Water Works there. George was having a hard time settling down to civilian life doing speculative building, for he was nostalgic for army days in spite of wounds or imprisonment. Walt's mother complained to Walt that George was becoming tight with money, and guessed that he was thinking of getting married. Walt was now affluent enough to lend George five hundred dollars on a real estate investment.

As for Walt's job, he found it very congenial, especially as he was free to use the office in the evenings and sit there in the warmth, his work pages illuminated by "a splendid astral lamp, to burn gas by a tube . . . ," writing or reading as long as he wished.

In July, William Michael Rossetti, English scholar and critic, brother of the poet, Dante Gabriel Rossetti, wrote a very favorable criticism of the *Leaves.* The review was reprinted in American papers. When, in 1868, Rossetti put out an English edition of Whitman's work, it was the beginning of Whitman's fame abroad. Within a year or two his work was being read in the English universities, and critics who were rebelling against prudery and hypocrisy in Great Britain hailed him as an outstanding voice of the New World. Among the enthusiastic was Algernon Charles Swinburne, whose own poetry was savagely attacked for its sensuality and pessimism. Written in highly musical, skilled rhymes, his poetry was very unlike Whitman's, but Swinburne appreciated the American bard's vigor and even compared him favorably to the great English poet William Blake. The elegy to Abraham Lincoln he called "the most sweet and sonorous nocturne ever chanted in the church of the world."

The "good gray poet" began to find his humble living quarters the goal of an increasing number of distinguished English visitors eager to see and hear him in person. As for his own countrymen, they were still largely indifferent, if not hostile. When the first edition of the *Leaves* had appeared twelve years earlier, one reviewer had hoped the book would disappear and die. But now it was sprouting new buds and branches, each volume thicker than the one before.

"In my own country, so far," Whitman wrote to an English critic and champion, "from the press and from authoritative quarters, I have received but one long tirade of impudence, mockery and scurrilous jeers. Only since the English recognition have the skies here lighted up a little."

He should have underlined the word "little" for in America there were more clouds and storm than light. But Walt was a "free old hawk" still, as he told Pete Doyle, preferring ferry boats, Broadway, and country rambles to tea cups and stuffy parlors, or even the companionship of a few intellectuals who began to gather around him.

He remained the searcher and singer who had written, "I wear my hat as I please indoors or out . . . I refuse putting from me what I really am."

8

Steer for the Deep Waters Only

Although the North and the South had been torn apart by war and were still by no means unified in spirit in the years of contention and reconstruction that followed, the eastern and western parts of the United States were dramatically bound together on May 10, 1869. On that day, on a barren promontory at Ogden, Utah, workmen, executives in top hats, women in billowy gowns, celebrated the completion of a railroad that bound East and West together by a band of steel. Across 1,800 miles, from Missouri to the Pacific, over plunging canyons and rugged ledges, through deserts darkened by herds of buffalo, past buttes and mesas where resentful Indians threatened, the rails of the Union Pacific and the Central Pacific stretched without a break.

Walt Whitman's dream of a transcontinental railroad, a dream shared by nearly every other American of his time, became a fact. No more would the lumbering overland stages lurch across prairie and desert, or settlers have to rely on creeping oxdrawn wagons. Now they could ride in comparative comfort from New York to California in the then astonishing time of only six and a half days.

The whole world was being bound more closely together, for in the same year the Suez Canal was finally completed, joining the Mediterranean and the Red Sea, thus making a new, great channel for ships traveling between Europe and Asia. And only three years before, a permanent cable was finally strung across the floor of the Atlantic Ocean, uniting the New World with the Old.

With these engineering marvels changing the whole tempo of life, and with America buzzing with expansion, new trades, lumbering, mining, commerce, and new states sprouting up in what had once been wilderness, it is no wonder that Whitman found himself searching for poetic lines to encompass all of the scene. He succeeded and in this period produced one of his finest poems, "Passage to India," which begins:

> Singing my days,
> Singing the great achievements of the present,
> Singing the strong light works of engineers,
> Our modern wonders (the antique ponderous Seven outvied,)
> In the Old World the east the Suez Canal,
> The New by its mighty railroad spann'd,
> The seas inlaid with eloquent gentle wires . . .

Let more popular poets continue to write about Greece and Rome and the wonders of the ancient world. Walt spoke for the world as it was—though he was by no means indifferent to the glories of the past and man's long search to find a passage to India, the "struggles of many a captain, tales of many a sailor dead . . ." He proclaims that he celebrates not only "facts of modern science" but the myths and fables of Asia and Africa as well, "The deep diving bibles and legends, The daring plots of the poets, the elder religions," affirming, "You too with joy I sing." Yet it is the present, with its mechanical progress, which gives him a symbol for the hoped-for, increasing closeness of all mankind.

> I see over my own continent the Pacific railroad surmounting every barrier,
> I see continual trains of cars winding along the Platte carrying freight and passengers,
> I hear the locomotives rushing and roaring, and the shrill steam-whistle,
> I hear the echoes reverberate through the grandest scenery in the world,
> I cross the Laramie plains, I note the rocks in grotesque shapes, the buttes,
> I see the plentiful larkspur and wild onions, the barren, colorless, sage-deserts
>
> Marking through these and after all, in duplicate slender lines,
> Bridging the three or four thousand miles of land travel,
> Tying the Eastern to the Western sea,
> The road between Europe and Asia.

Whitman had traveled no farther west than St. Louis, Missouri, at this time, but he saw "the Laramie plains . . . the Wind River and the Wahsatch mountains . . . the Humboldt Range . . . the clear waters of Lake Tahoe . . . the forests of majestic pines . . . the alkaline plains" with their "enchanting mirages of waters and meadows" in imagination. He is not talking in his poem of actual travel only, but of the travels of the soul. He is singing "not for trade or transportation only, But in God's name, and for thy sake O soul."

O soul, repressless, I with thee and thou with me,
Thy circumnavigation of the world begin . . .

O we can wait no longer,
We too take ship O soul,
Joyous we too launch out on trackless seas . . .

"Passage to more than India!" Whitman proclaims. "Steer for the deep waters only . . . For we are bound where mariner has not yet dared to go, And we will risk the ship, ourselves and all."

O farther farther sail!
O daring joy, but safe! are they not all the seas of God?
O farther, farther, farther sail!

Whitman was fifty years old at the time he worked on this poem, no longer the robust, healthy man who had started the exhausting work of wound dresser and comrade to Civil War soldiers. Vacationing at Brooklyn in August, 1869, he found himself envying George's vigor and writing about it to O'Connor. "He was out in all the excessive heat of the three latter days of last week and came home every evening to his supper, unflagging, and full of strength and fun—I quite envied and admired him —especially as I felt deathly weak—indeed despicable." September was cooler, but even then Whitman wrote to Peter Doyle about continued spells of dizziness and sudden sweat.

Yet he was still writing vigorous poetry and planning another edition of his *Leaves of Grass*, as if he could never cease tinkering with it, adding and revising, shifting the sequence of the poems, increasingly conscious that this one book was his life's work. In spite of his government post, there was a constant drain on his income, not only by his mother and Edward but by his charities toward the sick or to Doyle and other workmen when they were unemployed. His living quarters in Washington were still of the humblest kind, his room containing only a bed, a shaky washstand, two or three rickety chairs, and a writing desk that staggered on its weak legs. Everything, as usual, was strewn with newspapers, clippings, poems, and letters.

Among the latter was one that William Rossetti had sent to O'Connor, enclosing comments on Whitman's poetry made by an Englishwoman, identified only as a wife and mother. The woman's praise was extravagant. The reading of Whitman's poems, she said, gave her truly a new birth of the soul. "I had not dreamed that words could cease to be words, and become electric streams like these . . . I am as one hurried through stormy seas, over high mountains, dazed with sunlight, stunned with a crowd and tumult of faces and voices, till I am breathless, bewildered, half dead."

In December, 1869, Whitman wrote to Rossetti, although his letter was intended for the unknown woman as well. "I am deeply touched by these sympathies and convictions coming from a woman and from England . . ." Such comments coming from "the heart and conscience of a true wife and mother" had given him much comfort, he wrote. He enclosed two photographs of himself which showed him in his broad-brimmed hat and open collar. "One is intended for the lady (if I may be permitted to send it her)—and will you please accept the other, with my respects and love?" He added that he was feeling quite well and hearty in spite of his complaints about his health earlier in the fall.

The lady who received Walt's portrait was a brown-haired, attractive, and warm-hearted woman, Anne Gilchrist, who, eight years previously, had been widowed, at age thirty-three. She had been left with four children, and also an unfinished biography of the poet William Blake that her husband had been working on. She finished this herself, proving her own literary abilities. A woman with a deeply religious nature, she responded not only to Whitman's poetry but to him as a man, and her passion for his poetry was transferred to him as an individual. Soon she was to start a personal correspondence with him, pouring out her love and devotion in words that took Walt by surprise.

Whitman protested to an English visitor that his friends in England had gone too far in praising him. Anne Gilchrist's lavish praise, her lengthy comments printed in their entirety as *A Woman's Estimate of Walt Whitman* in a Boston newspaper, was gratifying, but even this was more like a love letter than a critical review. Still, as Whitman later said, "You can imagine what such a thing as her 'Estimate' meant to me at that time. Almost everybody was against me . . . I had got so used to being ignored or denounced that the appearance of a friend was always accompanied by a sort of shock." He was grateful to this "wonderful woman," but he had no thought or desire for a romantic relationship with her.

He had problems much closer to home. On March 21, 1870, Walt received word from the insane asylum that his brother Jesse was dead. He had to write his mother this grim news.

His mother replied in her characteristic semi-literate way, "O Walt aint it sad to think the poor soul hadent a friend near him in his last moments . . . i was thinking of him more lately than common . . . i feel very sad of course Walt if he has done ever so wrong he was my first born but gods will be done

good bie Walter dear"

In May, Whitman cut his thumb badly. When it became infected, he could not hold a pen and had to take a leave from his job for some weeks. By June he had recovered enough to be able to jot down mysterious notes to himself in his notebook, notes that indicate a very agitated emotional and intellectual state, with references to an anonymous individual. On one page he resolved "TO GIVE UP ABSOLUTELY and for good, from this present hour, this FEVERISH, FLUCTUATING, useless undignified pursuit of 164—too long, (much too long) persevered in,—so humiliating . . . avoid seeing her, or meeting her, or any talk or explanation —" Walt was not the serene, radiant, saint figure that O'Connor had painted, but was in the grip of an "incessant, enormous perturbation," and was keenly dissatisfied with himself.

In July, Whitman took an extended leave from his job, employing another worker as his replacement, and went home to Brooklyn. He wanted partly to escape the heat, his own agitated state of mind, and to prepare his new edition of *Leaves of Grass* and a prose work called *Democratic Vistas*. Since his mother and Eddie were alone now, Jeff in St. Louis and George in Camden, there was room for Walt in the house, and he spent four or five hours a day reading proofs there before going off to his favorite enjoyments in New York or the Long Island shore. When he went back to Washington in October, his new volumes were being bound.

The 1871, or fifth, edition of his poems met with almost total silence on the part of the critics. Actually, except for "Passage to India," the newness consisted chiefly in rearranging the sequence of the poems. England was still his main source of reassurance, although in August he was cheered by being invited to write and read a poem celebrating the fortieth National Industrial Exhibition in New York City. In September, Walt appeared and read the poem he had written especially for the occasion. He could scarcely make himself heard above the noise of hammers and saws since workmen were still busy arranging exhibits. What newspaper critics did hear, and see, they quickly made known by sarcastic and jeering comments in the news media, sneering both at the poem—which was not a good one—and at Walt's mannerisms. Hurt and baffled, Walt turned again to his English admirers.

He bundled off the new *Leaves* to Rossetti and to Anne Gilchrist. Mrs. Gilchrist responded with her first personal letter which, though it may have helped heal Whitman's wounds, must have made him feel some apprehension over her ardor.

After describing her marriage, then the anguish of losing her husband and the trials of raising her beloved children by herself, she mentioned her first reading of Whitman's book. It was, she said, "the voice of my Mate" speaking. "Never yet has bride sprung into her husband's arms with the joy with which I would take thy hand and spring from the shore . . . O come. Come, my darling; look into these eyes and see the loving ardent aspiring soul in them." He is her "dear love," her "darling," and she is only waiting for time to unite them.

When Whitman did not answer, she wrote another letter in October, pleading for just one word from him.

Finally, in early November, Whitman replied. His letter was short and cautious, but he made every attempt to be warm. ". . . I am not insensible to your love. I too send you my love. And do you feel no disappointment because I now write but briefly. My book is my best letter . . . You understand this better and fuller and clearer than any one else . . . Enough that there surely exists between us so beautiful and delicate a relation, accepted by both of us with joy."

Again there was a long and ardent response from Anne Gilchrist, only one of many such letters that she was to write in the coming years. By all reports, including a biography of her written by her son, Herbert, Anne Gilchrist was a sensitive and even brilliant woman, a friend of Thomas Carlyle, George Eliot,

John Ruskin, and Alfred Tennyson. But, for whatever reason, she made Whitman into a kind of deity and out of her own yearnings all but demanded that he be not only her soul mate but husband. It was surely, as Whitman wrote, "a delicate relation," but he did his best to meet her at least halfway, and when later she came to the United States expressly to meet him and be with him, he enjoyed her company and that of her family. Eventually she realized that Walt was not interested in her except as a dear friend, and she accepted this with grace.

Anne Gilchrist was still a healthy and vigorous woman in 1871, but at age fifty-two Whitman's sieges of weakness and dizziness were increasing in number. In 1872 he left his clerkship three times for a total of three and a half months. Aside from ill health, he still had to play the role of peacemaker in his family. George had finally married, and he and his wife Louisa had established a home in Camden, New Jersey. They persuaded Walt's mother, whose health was increasingly bad, to move in with them. She was not at all happy in the new arrangement and complained often to Walt. But most painful of all of Walt's problems was the quarrel he and his longtime friend William O'Connor had over political differences at O'Connor's house.

O'Connor believed strongly that Negroes should be given the vote. Walt thought that they must be educated before being granted such responsibility. John Burroughs was present at O'Connor's home when the quarrel broke out. According to his report, the two men gored each other verbally like bulls—a common habit in their arguments—and at last O'Connor became enraged. Walt, insulted, took his hat and marched out. The next day he overcame his sense of injury enough so that when he and O'Connor happened to meet on the street, Walt held out his hand to his friend. O'Connor dodged past him and went on as if he not seen Walt.

The broken friendship was a loss to both men, and meant that Whitman could no longer enjoy the evenings at the O'Connor home, although Ellen O'Connor remained as friendly as before. Burroughs, Eldridge, and other friends were upset by the rift, but there was nothing to do but accept it for as long as it might last.

Whitman was hurt and disappointed in another way that same year. Swinburne, who had praised his poetry, had even gone so far as to title one of his own poems "To Walt Whitman An American." Now, toward the end of 1872, Walt learned that Swinburne had cooled toward him and his poetry, partly because Whitman's defenders, such as Rossetti and Robert Buchanan, were too ardent. Actually, Swinburne's criticism was not hot-headed and was, in part, accurate. Whitman was at his best, according to Swinburne, when he spoke for himself. "What he says is well said when he speaks of himself and because he cannot choose but speak; whether he speak of a small bird's loss or a great man's death, of a nation rising for battle or a child going forth in the morning." But Swinburne found too much of the propagandist in Whitman and ended his criticism by saying, "Never before was high poetry so puddled and adulterated with mere doctrine in its crudest form."

Whitman remained outwardly cheerful, but inwardly some old wounds were festering. Swinburne's remarks did not help his growing sense of being persecuted. He was aware, too, that in spite of his success in "Passage to India" his poetic vigor was slackening. Also, he was increasingly disturbed by ill health. The doctors he consulted did not accurately diagnose his trouble, which was hypertension, commonly called high blood pressure, and so he continued to drive himself in his work, to live as freely as he always had, and to fret over his lack of appreciation by the American public. In his *Democratic Vistas* he again acclaimed his belief in the underlying value of democracy, but he expressed his dismay at the contemporary scene:

> Never was there, perhaps, more hollowness at heart than at present, and here in the United States. Genuine belief seems to have left us. The underlying principles of the States are not honestly believed in . . . nor is humanity itself believed in. What penetrating eye does not everywhere see through the mask? . . . We live in an atmosphere of hypocrisy throughout. The men believe not in the women, nor the women in the men. A scornful superciliousness rules in literature . . . The great cities reek with respectable as much as non-respectable robbery and scoundrelism. In fashionable life, flippancy, tepid amours, weak infidelism, small aims, or no aims at all, only to kill time. In business (this all-devouring modern word, business), the one sole object is, by any means, pecuniary gain.

Whitman has been accused of being a blind idealist in his praises of America and its people. He never lost faith, but he was a realist. He was well acquainted, through his political activity, with the actual workings of political parties, the compromises often required, or the outright betrayals of principle. He knew intimately the so-called common people, and though he celebrated human beings en masse, it was the individual person with whom he was concerned. The job of government, he said, was essentially to help individuals to rule themselves and to encourage the development of the central beauty and potentiality of each individual soul. Democracy did not mean anarchy. It had its own laws, he reminded his countrymen, "of the strictest and amplest kind. Many suppose . . . that it means a throwing aside of law, and running riot."

Even if democracy in America were realized, it would only be a beginning. ". . . it alone can bind, and ever seeks to bind, all nations, all men, of however various and distant lands, into a brotherhood, a family. It is the old, yet ever-modern dream of earth, out of her eldest and her youngest, her fond philosophers and poets. Not that half only, individualism which isolates. There is another half, which is the adhesiveness of love, that fuses, ties, and aggregates, making the races comrades, and fraternizing all." Today, his words have a special ring of truth and warning. "Of all dangers to a nation . . . there can be no greater one than having certain portions of the people set off from the rest by a line drawn—they not privileged as others, but degraded, humiliated, made of no account."

In his book he called again for great poets in the United States, "poets not only possessed of the religious fire and abandon of Isaiah, luxuriant in the epic talent of Homer, or for proud characters as in Shakespeare, but consistent with the Hegelian formulas, and consistent with modern science. America needs, and the world needs, a class of bards who will, now and ever, so link and tally the rational physical being of man, with the ensembles of time and space, and with this fast and multiform show, Nature, surrounding him, ever tantalizing him, equally a part, and yet not a part of him, as to essentially harmonize, satisfy, and put at rest."

It was a very tall order. He had hoped to be that poet, and still desired to be.

Around this time he wrote to Anne Gilchrist that she should not imagine that he was the half-divine person and poet she had constructed in her imagination. "The actual W.W.," he told her, "is a very plain personage and entirely unworthy such devotion." This is a modest note for Walt Whitman. It may have been a product of ill health and depression, or perhaps it was just an attempt to counter Mrs. Gilchrist's excessive adulation.

On the night of January 23, 1873, Whitman walked to his office in the Treasury Building as he often did, to enjoy its comforts and the bright gas lamp. On this night, with rain and sleet ticking against the window, he relaxed beside the bright fire and sat lazily reading one of the books at hand. He was distracted from reading by a general feeling of physical uneasiness and several times pushed the book away. But he stayed on, trying to ignore his feeling of illness, so that it was quite late before he finally left. At the door of the Treasury, the guard looked at him with concern and asked him what was wrong, saying that he looked ill. The guard offered to find someone to take his place while he helped Whitman to his lodgings which were only about a hundred yards down the street.

"No," Whitman said. "I can go well enough."

The guard insisted. Again Whitman declined his help and started off. The guard followed him down the steps and then stood holding his lantern high so that its rays would help Whitman find his way through the wet, cold darkness.

Whitman reached his attic room, undressed, and went to bed. Around three or four in the morning he woke and discovered that he could not move his left arm or leg. But he felt no pain, not even any general discomfort. Perhaps, he hoped, it was only a temporary condition. He tried to dismiss any undue anxiety and went back to sleep.

It was daylight when he opened his eyes again and started to get out of bed. He could not move. His whole left side was without sensation, paralyzed. Helpless, he lay on the bed in the bleak, littered little room, waiting for someone to come.

Several hours passed before there was a knock at the door.

131

"Some friends came in," Whitman wrote later, "and they immediately sent for a doctor—fortunately a very good one, Dr. W. B. Drinkard. He looked very grave—thought my condition markedly serious. I did not think so: I supposed the attack would pass off soon—but it did not."

Whitman had suffered a stroke. Bedridden, he was in need of the close friends he had made, and they quickly volunteered help: Pete Doyle, Ursula Burroughs, Ellen O'Connor, Charles Eldridge, and the wife of J. Hubley Ashton, the man who had helped to procure a government job for Whitman. Mrs. Ashton wanted to move Walt to her own home, but he clung to his familiar room. The thought of being with the Ashtons, who lived on such a grand scale compared to him, with servants and many luxuries, had no appeal for Walt. He had never cared for what he called "little extra fixings and superfluities," in health, and he did not need them in sickness.

Although in a few days he was able to sit up in bed, propped with pillows, and scribble a reassuring note to his mother, he was still bedfast at the end of the month, and still unable to move without dizziness or nausea. He had many callers, he wrote her, and everything in the way of comfort that he needed.

"I have a good bed—a fire—as much grub as I wish and whatever I wish—and two or three good friends here. So I want you to not feel at all uneasy—as I write Peter Doyle is sitting by the window reading—he and Charles Eldridge regularly come in and do whatever I want and are both *very helpful* to me . . ."

He remained optimistic, believing that he would surely, though slowly, regain the power to walk. As for what had caused the paralytic stroke, the doctor suggested that it had been the result of emotional disturbances that he had experienced. His friends believed that it was a result of exposure to the various infections in the military hospitals and his arduous activities there. According to Walt's own account in *Specimen Days* he had made over six hundred visits or tours to hospital, camp, or field, and befriended some eighty thousand to a hundred thousand of the wounded and sick. His visits varied from an hour or two to all day or night. Those three years he considered "the greatest privilege" as well as "the most profound lesson" of his life. But there was no doubt that they had taken their toll of his strength, and it was at the beginning of his war service that he had had his first disquieting symptoms of hypertension.

Whatever the cause, the magnificent health he had known so long was gone. But not his will to live. He had written years before, in "Song of Myself," "And as to you Death, and you bitter hug of mortality, it is idle to try to alarm me."

9

This Savage Shore

Early in February, 1873, Walt Whitman, supported on each side by Peter Doyle and another friend, hobbled down the four flights of stairs from his room as far as the street. It was a triumph, but an exhausting one that left him feeling much worse the next day, although he was still certain of his eventual recovery.

It was no help to Whitman's own health progress that the sister-in-law he was very fond of, Jeff's wife, Martha, was fighting a losing battle against tuberculosis of the lungs. On February 19th, to Walt's great grief, he received a telegram from his brother Jeff that Martha had died that day. Although on the day of "Matty's" funeral Walt felt strong enough to struggle up and down the stairs again, he kept thinking of her more than of himself.

Dr. Drinkard was trying electric battery stimulation on Walt's numbed limbs, but with no great success. Much better for Walt's spirits was a carriage ride which Ursula Burroughs took him on. John Burroughs was in New York, working as a government bank inspector, and planning on building a new home in Roxbury, where he had grown up. His letters pressed his wife for news of Walt, and in April Walt wrote to his good friend. He was by then able to spend a couple of hours at his office desk although he admitted, "I am still in a pretty bad way." But he would, he declared, get as well as ever in time. He hoped to go and live in Camden with his mother and George, but he did not want to leave Washington until he was able to move around more freely. In his room, he said, there was a cluster of lilacs in a pitcher—those flowers that always reminded him of Abraham Lincoln.

He continued to write cheerful letters to his mother, who was increasingly unhappy living with George and his wife "Lou." Walt held out the dream of building or buying a little house in Washington for her, himself, and Edward. His mother clung to this idea and hope, but she was more and more ill with what she believed were stomach troubles. She was now seventy-three years old, nervous, discontented, and failing. Seriously ill in early May, she improved enough to write to Walt on May 16th, telling him not to be worried and not to come to Camden until he felt much better and could walk without too much effort.

A few days later she had a relapse and Walt managed to get to Camden only three days before his mother's death on May 20th.

Whitman felt keenly the loss of the woman he had once called "a perfect mother." Her death, that of Martha, and the memory of President Lincoln bore down upon him as he returned to Washington a week later to arrange for an indefinite leave of absence. Since even his familiar room depressed him, he accepted the invitation of the Ashtons to share their home, and moved there for a week or two. Eldridge was shocked at his general condition, and wrote to John Burroughs about it. Walt was a physical wreck, he confided, in comparison to what he had been, and could not walk even a block without resting. It was pitiful, Eldridge said, and he was afraid that Walt might have another attack. The only bright spot was that he seemed to be mentally as vigorous as ever and clung to his belief in his eventual recovery.

After making arrangements for a substitute on his government job, Walt packed his trunk, with Doyle's help, stored a few possessions with friends, and went back to his brother's house in Camden. He did not plan to stay long, but even a few days there made him feel deeply lonely. George and he had never had much in common, and although his sister-in-law was kind and considerate, Walt missed his Washington friends and his former independence. To Doyle he wrote letters in which he outlined unrealistic plans for trips they might take together by steamboat or train, anywhere within sight of water and shore. George's house was near a railroad, and Walt could hear "the bells and whistles and trains rumbling continually, night and day," carrying passengers where he had not the strength to go.

He wrote, too, to Anne Gilchrist, telling her of his stroke and his bereavement. "I am up and dressed every day, sleep and eat middling well and do not change much yet, in flesh and face, only look very old . . . I walk with difficulty and have to stay in the house nearly all the time . . . I feel that I shall probably get well—though I may not.

"Many times during the past year have I thought of you and your children."

Although his plans were not definite, he hoped to go back to Washington after the hot season was over, he told her.

He sent his love to her and her children and enclosed a ring which he took from his own finger. Perhaps he thought this token would satisfy her desire for some more concrete evidence of affection from him, since he could not honestly encourage her romantic hopes in words. Also, in spite of his outward optimism, he must have had doubts about his eventual recovery, for he had drawn up a will, and sincerely wanted her to have the remembrance of the ring.

Mrs. Gilchrist took the ring to mean more than Walt had intended and responded that she was now entirely satisfied and at peace. She would wear the ring for as long as she drew breath. Her only sorrow was that she could not be near to care for him in his sickness.

A visit from Burroughs, in October, helped to break Walt's loneliness. And though he was able to hobble around a bit more, he still remained in Camden in November and December. When the weather was good he managed short trips to visit a neighboring colonel whom he took a liking to, and also rode the horse-cars in Camden and Philadelphia. Letter carriers, conductors, and drivers helped him on and off, and were willing to provide the talk and friendship he needed. He began to write again, poetry and articles for the newspapers.

He was still in Camden at the beginning of the New Year, and had begun a series of articles for a weekly newspaper based on the notes he had made during the war. New poems, too, were forming in his mind. He wrote one to a California giant sequoia, called "Song of the Redwood-Tree," though he had never seen such a tree. He had read about them, however, and he identified himself with "a mighty dying tree in the redwood forest dense." He hears the voice of the dying tree: "Farewell my brethren, Farewell O earth and sky, farewell ye neighboring waters, My time has ended, my term has come." This was actually the voice of Walt Whitman speaking out of his solitude. Against the melancholy and resignation to eventual death, he looked forward to the "superber race" that would follow both the tree and him. The past would nourish the future, one of his repeated themes.

Another poem of the time expressed even more intimately his thoughts about age and death. Although he called the poem "Prayer of Columbus," he might as well have called it Prayer of Walt Whitman—as he more or less said to Ellen O'Connor.

A batter'd, wreck'd old man,
Thrown on this savage shore, far, far from home . . .

Camden was no savage shore, but it seemed alien enough to
Whitman. He—identifying with Columbus—addressed God di-
rectly:

Thou knowest my years entire, my life,
My long and crowded life of active work, not adoration
    merely;
Thou knowest the prayers and vigils of my youth,
Thou knowest my manhood's solemn and visionary medi-
    tations,
Thou knowest how before I commenced I devoted all to
    come to Thee

O I am sure they really came from Thee,
The urge, the ardor, the unconquerable will

Old, poor, and paralyzed, I thank Thee.

Whitman was still in Camden in March, 1874, but he planned
to return to his government job, or hoped to. He had been, at his
request, transferred to the office of the Solicitor of the Treasury.
During his absence he had been paying a substitute to work for
him, but as his salary was higher than what he had to pay the
substitute, he had some money left over. In June, hearing that
certain government employees were going to be let go, he wrote
to President Grant, asking to be kept on in his clerkship. It did
not help, for the Government was in an economy mood and at
the end of June Whitman was notified that his job would end

as of July 1st, although he would receive two additional months' pay.

So he was cut off from even the little financial security his income had provided. He turned to the only immediate source of money he had, aside from his meager savings, and became a newspaper writer again, hoping to earn enough to pay his board and that of Edward, who had been sent to live with a family in the country.

Loneliness was assuaged chiefly by letters from his old friends. Burroughs was busily working on his house on the Hudson eighty miles north of New York City, and kept Walt informed of his progress and of his beehives. A room was ready for Walt any time he could come, Burroughs said, and the breakfast plate warmed.

Walt longed to accept the invitation, but he did not feel up to it. And for all that he wrote to Doyle about his loneliness, he was keeping busy not only with newspaper work and new poems but was planning yet another edition of *Leaves of Grass*. He wanted to publish it in 1876 in conjunction with the Centennial Exposition at Philadelphia that was being prepared to celebrate the first century of the American Republic.

This time he planned to publish his work in two volumes; *Leaves of Grass* in one, the second volume to contain new poems together with prose, to be called *Two Rivulets*, and he was working on a preface for the latter volume.

"At the eleventh hour, under grave illness," he began, "I gather up the pieces of Prose and Poetry left over since publishing, a while since, my first and main volume, LEAVES OF GRASS—pieces, here, some new, some old—nearly all of them (sombre as many are, making this almost Death's book) composed in by-gone atmosphere of perfect health." He was sending these out, he said, as "my contribution and outpouring to celebrate, in some sort, the feature of the time, the first Centennial of our New World Nationality . . . the mother of many coming Centennials."

He paused in the writing of the main preface to take time for a long footnote. "As I write these lines, May 31, 1875, it is again early summer—again my birthday—now my fifty-sixth. Amid the outside beauty and freshness, the sunlight and verdure of the delightful season, O how different the moral atmosphere amid which I now revise this Volume, from the jocund influence surrounding the growth and advent of LEAVES OF GRASS. I occupy myself, arranging these pages for publication, still enveloped in thoughts of the death two years since of my dear Mother . . . and also under the physical affliction of a tedious attack of paralysis, obstinately lingering and keeping its hold upon me . . ."

He carefully tried to describe what he had meant to say in his *Leaves,* and what the book meant to him. It had received its impetus, he said, from the spirit of Democracy and the perennial influences of Nature—"the strong air of prairie and mountains, the dash of the briny sea, the primary antiseptics—of the passions, in all their fullest heat and potency, of courage, rankness, amativeness, and immense pride. . . ." But he worried whether the *moral* intentions had been fully grasped. Also, he made it clear that he meant his *Leaves* to be "the Poem of Identity, (of Yours, whoever you are, now reading these lines) . . ."

In the fall, November, Whitman was pleased and surprised by a visit from an Englishman, Lord Houghton. Since Walt's sister-in-law was still in bed, having just borne a child whom she and George had named for Walt, he had to play host alone. Lord Houghton had been visiting the literary lights of Boston and Concord, including Emerson, and he told Whitman that Emerson was as loyal to him as ever. This was reassuring as Whitman had been hurt when, two years before, Emerson had published an anthology of poetry without including any lines of his. The other prominent authors—Longfellow, Lowell, and Oliver Wendell Holmes—had tried to prevent Houghton's visiting Walt, whom they still considered a disgrace to American letters. Whitman and the aristocratic Englishman enjoyed each other, Whitman as casual as if he were entertaining a visitor from next door. Whitman searched around the kitchen for a snack to offer the visitor, but could find nothing except some baked apples. When George came home from work, he was embarrassed to find Walt and his distinguished visitor calmly dining on the sparse fare, but Whitman was as unperturbed as if he had presented Houghton with a full meal.

Not long after this, Whitman felt well enough to make a visit to Washington. He had a chance to see numerous old friends, but not William O'Connor, who still avoided him. In England, other friends, including Anne Gilchrist, were concerned about Walt's economic welfare. Since he was obviously going to have to publish his sixth edition of his poems by himself—no commercial publisher was willing—the English group decided to pledge themselves individually to purchasing copies of the two-volume set. Many distinguished English citizens, including Tennyson, the Rossettis, and Lord Houghton, subscribed. It was a boost to Whitman's morale and promised to add to his meager bank account.

Even so, the winter months of confinement in Camden, the many days indoors, were frustrating and depressing to a man who had once been able to walk or ride in any weather. With spring came an increased longing for the countryside and sometime in early April or early May, 1876, Whitman went to live at the house of some new friends who had a farm about twelve miles from Camden. The owners of the place were George and Susan Stafford, parents of a boy who worked in the printing office where Walt was now having his new books set in type. Walt had made friends with young Harry Stafford, and the boy had taken him to visit the farm which overlooked a willow-draped stream, Timber Creek. George Stafford was a religious man and a faithful Methodist, but he apparently saw no harm in having the bearded poet as a guest, or he was influenced by his wife, who felt a bond of sympathy and affection for the crippled Whitman.

The pastoral loveliness of the place, the lilac bushes and maples, oaks and poplars, the glimpses of the creek sparkling four hundred yards below the homestead, renewed Whitman's determination to enjoy nature again as he had so often in the past. The creek, strong and clear, became his goal. At first he ventured only a short way outdoors, pausing to rest and bask in the sunlight. Besides Harry, there were six other Stafford children, and several often followed Walt about, carrying a light chair for him to sit in when he grew tired. Little by little he increased the distance he could travel toward his sparkling goal, and in several weeks he managed to cover the route.

It was the beginning of one of the happiest periods of Whitman's life, a time when he could truly loaf and look and marvel, and fill his notebooks with page after page of nature descriptions.

"Dear, soothing, healthy, restoration hours—after three confining years of paralysis—after the long strain of the war, and its wounds and death."

It was joy simply to walk down the farm lane. "As every man has his hobby-liking, mine is for a real farm lane fenced by old chestnut rails gray-green with dabs of moss and lichen, copious weeds and briers growing in spots athwart the heaps of stray-picked stones at the fence bases—irregular paths worn between, and horse and cow tracks . . . apple tree blossoms in forward April—pigs, poultry, a field of August buckwheat, and in another the long flapping tassels of maize—and so to the pond, the expansion of the creek, the secluded-beautiful, with young and old trees, and such recesses and vistas."

There he bathed, in sunlight as well as in water, in a stream "thick as my neck, pure and clear . . . always gurgling ceaselessly—meaning, saying something, of course (if one could only translate it)—always gurgling there, the whole year through" among "oceans of mint, blackberries . . ."

After politics, wars, business, love, even friendship had been exhausted, there always remained nature. If anything could heal him, the world of nature could.

May was a month not only of swarming and mating birds but also "bumblebee month." He loved to watch the "crooning, hairy insects" as he hobbled down to the creek. "As I wend slowly along, I am often accompanied with a moving cloud of them," he wrote in the notebooks that were to become a part of his *Specimen Days*. "They play a leading part in my morning, midday or sunset rambles . . . Large and vivacious and swift, with wonderful momentum and a loud swelling, perpetual hum, varied now and then by something almost like a shriek, they dart to and fro, in rapid flashes, chasing each other, and (little things as they are) conveying to me a new and pronounced sense of strength, beauty, vitality, a movement."

A log or stump, a fence rail, a hummock under a great tulip tree by the brook, all made comfortable seats for him while he wrote. Everything went into his notes, the sheen of grass and flower, the fragrance and movement of the air, the odors of cedar and oak, even the great patches of potatoes thriving on the farm, the sword-shaped calamus leaves by the pond, the singing of a single locust whose song "gushes, has meaning, is masculine, is like some fine old wine, not sweet, but far better than sweet."

He set down careful descriptions, often working more like a naturalist than a poet, listing and describing twenty kinds of trees that grew in the vicinity. At the same time he found a philosophic "lesson" in the very existence of a tree. "One lesson from affiliating a tree—perhaps the greatest moral lesson anyhow from earth, rock, animals—is that same lesson of inherency, of what *is*, without the least regard to what the looker-on (the critic) supposes or says, or whether he likes or dislikes."

His poems, too, existed. They existed whether people liked them or not. And he would continue to publish them, whether the critics liked them or not—critics who dismissed those who did champion Whitman's work as "hot little prophets."

John Burroughs had been sarcastically referred to as one of these. Burroughs had been one of the first to recognize Whitman's genius, especially in his first book, *Notes on Walt Whitman as Poet and Person,* published in 1867. The years in between had not changed Burroughs' opinion, and stung by attacks against Walt, he again came to the poet's defense in a long letter to the editor of the New York *Tribune,* dated March 30, 1876.

"I have no more doubt of his greatness than I have of the sun at noonday . . ." His poems "are a breath from the sea and the woods, and not from the libraries, and will be valued highest by him whose spiritual lungs are strongest and cleanest . . . It is a kind of disloyalty to Nature to say Whitman has no form. He has not form as a house, or a shield, or a heart, or a molder's pattern . . . or a dainty bit of verse by Longfellow has form; but he has form as a tree, a river, the clouds, a cataract, a flash of lightning . . . and this is all the form he aims at."

Walt had other champions, too. Anne Gilchrist was still passionately devoted. She continued to write long, fervent letters

144

—in January, 1876, she had written of her plans to come to America and rent a house for herself and her children—and Walt had tried to discourage her, vaguely promising that perhaps someday he could travel to London. But Mrs. Gilchrist was not to be put off and wrote in May that she was taking passage on one of the steamers that traveled straight to Philadelphia, sailing about September 1st. Her daughter Beatrice wanted to enroll in the medical school at the University of Pennsylvania, while Herbert was intent on a career as an artist. It was her desire to expose her family to America, a country which must be great to have produced so great a poet, as well as to see and be with Whitman.

Mrs. Gilchrist arrived in September and met Whitman for the first time. Whether she came to Camden or he went to Philadelphia is not clear, and there is no record of what must have been a dramatic meeting—Whitman cautiously offering the love that is friendship, Mrs. Gilchrist anticipating so much more. He was to see her soon again, in the company of Burroughs, who came down in the same month to attend the Centennial. Burroughs wrote to his wife that Walt liked Mrs. Gilchrist and her family very much—as he did. She was a rosy woman without one gray hair, Burroughs said, and her daughters were as fresh and comely as their mother. It was Burroughs who went house-hunting with them. When a house was found, Mrs. Gilchrist set one room aside for Whitman's use whenever he visited and wanted to stay over. Burroughs thought the family would be a "godsend" to Walt. Walt himself looked forward to visits with them and in the following year and later, often had dinner with them, or stayed the night.

The younger daughter, Grace, left a description of a typical visit by Walt to their home. After dinner on a summer day, the group would move out onto the space below the steps of the house, Whitman in a bamboo rocking chair, the others circled about him. In spite of his dragging left leg and cane, he still had "a most majestic presence . . . He was dressed always in a complete suit of gray clothes with a large spotless white linen collar, his flowing white beard filling in the gap at his sunburnt throat." Although his hair and beard were snow-white his complexion was a "fine colour, and unwrinkled." The group listened while Whitman talked on various subjects or recited poems of Tennyson or Shakespeare. They listened also to his singing while he bathed or dressed, anything from "The Star Spangled Banner" to an operatic aria. The whole family liked him, and Anne Gilchrist came to realize that friendship was all that Whitman wanted from her—which she gave him loyally for the rest of her life.

At the time of the Gilchrists' arrival, Whitman was still at Timber Creek, and he stayed there during October. The days grew crisp, with frost in the mornings and brilliant sunsets. "I don't know what or how," he wrote, "but it seems to me mostly owing to these skies . . . I have had this autumn some wondrously contented hours—may I not say perfectly happy ones?" These hours were so happy that he was still at the farm in November, most of the time, though he made journeys to Camden and Philadelphia. In December, Jeff, with his two young daughters, came to Camden from St. Louis for a visit. The four took the train to the New Jersey shore and then went for a carriage drive over the hard-packed sand, fortified by coffee and a good breakfast. The "sedgy perfume" of the salt grass meadows and lagoons made Walt's nostrils widen, reminding him of the long-ago perfumes of the South Bay and Long Island. After the carriage ride, he walked off by himself along the beach, stumping along with the help of his cane, but feeling so exhilarated he believed he could have gone on for hours more. The whole view was his, "space, simple, unornamented space. Distant vessels and the far-off, just visible trailing smoke of an inward-bound steamer; more plainly, ships, brigs, schooners, in sight, most of them with every sail set to the firm and steady wind." Over all was the rustle of Indian grass, the sound of waves on the gray-white beach, a music that had always deeply affected him and found its way into the lapping, and sometimes booming, music of his own poems.

Although he had been excited about the Centennial Exhibition, he attended only once. Partly he was disappointed because he had hoped to be invited to be the official poet, whereas Bayard Taylor, a former friend, was chosen. Aside from that, he could not walk around very easily and visiting the exhibits was exhausting. The two-volume edition he had published in celebration of the Centennial fared as usual with American critics, but since his English friends were paying ten dollars and more per set, his economic situation was helped. Actually, he was not as much in want as some of his sympathizers believed. He had a comfortable home with George, paying "just the same as at an inn," and he was certainly not starving as was sometimes reported. He himself protested the exaggeration of his destitution saying that there was "a great rattling of dry bones . . . about my poverty." Mostly self-supporting from boyhood, he feared ending up dependent on others, especially on George and Lou, who helpful though they were, understood nothing about Walt's writing. George, an engineer, cared far more for pipes than for poems, Walt said truthfully.

But his life in these years was neither lonely nor unpleasant, especially as he continued to enjoy his excursions to the Stafford farm. In February, 1877, it was warm enough to take one of his vigorous baths at the pond. Stripped to the skin, he splashed and exercised by wrestling with a tough oak sapling, pulling and

147

pushing, breathing in the bright air. "After I wrestle with the tree awhile, I can feel its young sap and virtue welling up out of the ground and tingling through me from crown to toe . . . Then for addition and variety I launch forth in my vocalism; shout declamatory pieces, sentiments, sorrow, anger, etc . . . or inflate my lungs and sing the wild tunes and refrains I heard of the blacks down south or patriotic songs I learned in the army. I make the echoes ring, I tell you."

White-bearded, crippled, Walt Whitman was still singing the song of himself, even if only the owls and rushes heard, still sounding his "barbaric yawp" with a spiritually youthful vigor.

By August he felt physically renewed, following his daily routine at the dell off one side of a creek. "Never before did I get so close to Nature," he said, taking an "Adamic air bath and flesh brushing from head to foot." Undressing, but keeping an old straw hat on his head, and easy shoes on his feet, scrubbing his chest and sides and legs with a stiff-elastic brush until his skin turned crimson, then bathing, taking his time, rinsing in the spout of the stream where it entered the pool, then toweling himself dry and basking in the sunlight.

"Many such hours, from time to time, the last two summers —I attribute my partial rehabilitation largely to them. Some good people may think it is a feeble or half-cracked way of spending one's time and thinking. Maybe it is."

He did not care. It was *his* way . . . *his* poetry . . . *his* life. He meant to live it fully, as long as he possibly could.

10

I Have Had My Say

"Wild man," "half-cracked," "barbarian"—whatever he was called, the world was slowly beginning to make its way to Walt Whitman's door. Among his visitors and admirers in the summer of 1877 was a Dr. Richard Bucke, superintendent of an insane asylum in Ontario. Bucke, as a youth, had been a friend of two other young men who were the first to discover silver in Nevada. With them he made a trip across the Sierra Nevada in the days before the great silver rush at Virginia City. The three men battled winter blizzards and cold, and only Bucke managed to get through alive, though with one foot so badly frozen it had to be amputated. Returning to his native Canada, he worked his way through medical school and gained fame as a nerve specialist. An admirer of the *Leaves,* he called first on Whitman during the Centennial Exposition. He was so impressed by Whitman that he referred to the meeting as a turning point in his life. Both he and another visitor, a Western frontier poet, Joaquin Miller, were so extravagant in their reactions to Whitman that they spoke of him as a god instead of a man. From England came yet another admirer, Edward Carpenter, who had first read the *Leaves* as a student at Cambridge University and felt that it had changed his life. Then years later he was to write a long, unrhymed poem influenced by Whitman's verse and otherwise make a name for himself as an author. He had come to the United States to see Whitman and the authors centered around Boston. He thought that Whitman far outshone any of them, and the only thing he saw in America that seemed quite to match Whitman in spirit was the thundering Niagara Falls.

Although Longfellow, Lowell, Holmes, and the others shone less brightly in Carpenter's eyes than Whitman, they and their coterie were still the ruling influence in American literature. Their attitude generally was condescending if not contemptuous. The aging Emerson was still gentle in his references to the poet he had so enthusiastically greeted in 1855, but implied that he was disappointed in Whitman's poetic development.

In June, 1878, Whitman was a guest of new friends, the J. H. Johnstons, whose spacious home was on upper Fifth Avenue at Eighty-sixth Street in New York. At that time the area was still comparatively rural, quiet, breezy, open, with ample space, sky, and birds. Whitman was there at the time of the death of the distinguished editor and poet, William Cullen Bryant. Although Bryant had cooled toward Walt since his publication of the *Leaves,* he had been friendly and helpful in earlier times. A good walker like Whitman, he had taken many long rambles with Walt around Brooklyn, Bryant entertaining and educating Whitman by talking about his European travels. Whitman went to the funeral of "the good, stainless, noble old citizen and poet," accompanied by Bucke and Burroughs.

A few days later, Whitman, with the Johnstons' son Albert, who called him "Uncle Walt," took a steamboat up the Hudson and spent several days with the Burroughses at Riverby. In *Specimen Days,* Whitman recorded his enjoyment of the trip, his pleasure in picking currants and raspberries, his drives about the country roads with Burroughs, dips in the Hudson River, the evenings on the verandah talking.

Anne Gilchrist had moved to Concord, but during the fall her son Herbert spent a good deal of time with Whitman, painting his portrait.

The following spring, April 14, 1879, Whitman gave a public lecture in New York City on the death of Abraham Lincoln. The lecture had been arranged by friends, and started a tradition which was to continue irregularly through the next eleven years. A couple of months later, Anne Gilchrist left America for England. She and Walt said farewell to each other in the Johnstons' house on Fifth Avenue, withdrawing by themselves to the parlor, both seemingly deeply moved when they rejoined the other guests afterward. Though they did not know it, it was their last meeting, for Whitman was never to journey to England, and six years later the "great-hearted woman," as Burroughs called her, was dead.

That fall Whitman at last had the opportunity to take the kind of long Western trip of which he had dreamed, to see in actuality the plains and prairies, pastures and forests he had so often cataloged in his poems. From faraway Kansas, by way of a Philadelphia newspaper publisher, Colonel John Forney, came an invitation for Walt to be guest and visiting poet at the Kansas Quarter-Centennial celebration in Lawrence, Kansas. Here was a chance to see the West and also to visit his beloved brother Jeff in St. Louis. Walt made his preparations and on September 10th, he, Colonel Forney, and several others set off from West Philadelphia. They left at night and so Walt had his first experience of riding in a railroad sleeping car.

He found it a "fierce, weird pleasure to lie in my berth at night in the luxurious palace car, drawn by the mighty Baldwin . . .

It is late, perhaps midnight or after—distances joined like magic —as we speed through Harrisburg, Columbus, Indianapolis . . . with our loud whinnies thrown out from time to time, or trumpet blasts, into the darkness." There was an element of danger in it, he thought, but that only added zest. The danger was there since about two-thirds of the way to St. Louis the train collided with another one. Whitman mentioned no injuries, but the thirty-six hours the trip was to have taken proved to be considerably longer because of the delay so that he had time for only one night with Jeff in St. Louis.

Crossing the state of Missouri, he looked with wonder at the miles on miles of rolling prairies dotted here and there with trees. He had no doubt that Missouri was agriculturally superior to any other state, and he felt that he could live happily with the people.

Whitman and his fellow travelers had thought of stopping in Kansas City, but when they arrived they found a reception committee ready and waiting to take them on to Lawrence. At Lawrence, Whitman and Colonel Forney were guests at the home of Judge John P. Usher, formerly Secretary of the Interior under Lincoln. Both Kansas City and Lawrence were "large, bustling, half-rural, handsome cities," and Walt was so busy enjoying them that he was more sight-seer than poet, talking with the Judge's two sons whom he considered true westerners of the noblest type. In fact, he was so busy talking with the young men, who had gone with him to Topeka where he was scheduled to appear before a large audience, that he completely forgot to go—even though he had written a special speech for the occasion.

From Topeka he rode on to Denver and again marveled at the vastness and variety of his America. He was especially impressed with Denver and spent several days there, exploring, talking, ingesting the sights . . . the silver-smelting works, the stores with windows of plate glass, the fast horses in the streets, and big greyhound dogs for antelope hunting, the sweet taste of mountain trout. But better even than all this were the men, "three fourths of them large, able, calm, alert, American."

Equally inspiring was the scenery when the Rio Grande railroad went southward. Such steep grades and undulating curves, the train "squirming around corners, or up and down hills—far glimpses of a hundred peaks, titanic necklaces, stretching north and south . . ." The ruggedness of it all, the magnificent sweep of gorge and stream, massed clouds and various colored rocks, seemed like geographic expressions matching the ruggedness, sweep, and massiveness he had tried to express in his poetry. In all the "grim yet joyous elemental abandon," he found himself thinking more and more: "I have found the law of my own poems."

In contrast to the largeness of the landscape, he found "a silent little follower," a yellow-petaled wild flower that grew by the millions along his route, the coreopsis. There was almost too much to see, flocks of prairie hens, prairie dogs, herds of antelope, strange dry rivers, ant hills and buffalo wallows, cowboys herding their droves of cattle, "bright-eyed as hawks," the towns on the plains like ships on a sea, adobe houses and sunsets. If all those could be fused in a perfect poem!

It was an emotionally and physically exhausted Whitman who arrived back in St. Louis in October. Since he had over-expended both energy and funds, he settled down with Jeff to recuperate. Either for lack of money, or because he wanted to spend a long time with his brother, Walt remained for three months. At Christmas, John Burroughs sent Walt a gift of one hundred dollars from a friend who wished to remain anonymous—it was James T. Fields, who had published Walt's poetry in the *At-*

lantic Monthly some ten years before. With the money, Walt bought a train ticket and returned home.

But he had developed a taste for travel and after five months of rest in Camden and frequent trips to Timber Creek, he set off once more by train, this time to be a guest of his friend Dr. Bucke in London, Ontario. There, living with Bucke and his wife in a house surrounded by gardens and lawns, he went through the wards of the asylum and the detached cottages, and was impressed by the common humanity of the inmates. There was nothing markedly repulsive or hideous that he saw. He who had identified with all other kinds of unfortunate individuals, slave, tramp, or prostitute, accepted these demented persons as victims of mysterious circumstances and wrongs, but with "the same old blood—the same red running blood" that all human beings shared. The Canadian landscape he saw was as thrilling as that of the American West, and the young Canadians seemed just as hardy, democratic, and progressive. In time, he believed, they would become Americans, for he thought it inevitable that Canada would become part of the United States.

He was a mistaken prophet in this instance. As for his acceptance as a poet, he found on his return to Camden in September, 1880, that the articles being written about him were not too much different from those that had greeted his first publication of the *Leaves.* True, he had a growing number of distinguished and admiring visitors and Dr. Bucke was interested in writing his biography, but even some of his literary friends stumbled over the sexual element in certain of his poems. Nevertheless, there was some unbending. Longfellow had called on him a couple of years before, a call which Whitman returned when he gave a second lecture on Lincoln in April, 1881, in Boston. The newspapers gave a favorable report on the lecture, and some of the leading writers attended, among them William Dean Howells.

After Whitman's return home, he learned that a leading Boston publisher, James R. Osgood, was interested in bringing out a new edition of *Leaves of Grass*. With the exception of the young publishers, Thayer and Eldridge, this was the first commercial publisher who had approached Walt in sixteen years. After a good deal of correspondence between Whitman and Osgood, a contract was agreed upon. One thing that Whitman insisted on was that "the sexuality odes about which the original row was started" be included, unchanged.

The book was ready for printing by mid-August and Whitman went up to Boston to supervise the process, as well as to enjoy himself with old friends there, and to journey to Concord for a "long and blessed evening with Emerson." Emerson's once brilliant mind had dimmed with his seventy-eight years, so for the most part, Whitman just sat and looked at him quietly. In spite of the differences between the reserved and intellectual Emerson and the emotionally charged Whitman, there was a bond of sympathy between the two that, though it sometimes became frayed, never completely snapped. Emerson's shrewd and brilliant neighbor, Thoreau, had died long before at the comparatively young age of forty-five. Whitman paid his respects to the man he had known so briefly back in his Brooklyn days by carrying a stone to the memorial cairn at Thoreau's beloved Walden Pond.

Memories of President Lincoln's assassination were painfully revived during that weekend in Concord, for President James Garfield was reported to be in extreme danger as the result of an assassin's bullet the month before. When Whitman returned to Boston it was to the sound of bells tolling the news of Garfield's death on the night of September 19th. Garfield, whom Walt had know as a general and an ambitious politician in Washington, was a personal friend, and Whitman again felt bereft. He quickly wrote a poem and managed to insert it into the new edition of *Leaves,* describing the clang of the bells as "Those heart-beats of a Nation in the night."

Toward the end of October Whitman returned to Camden, awaiting the publication of the seventh edition of his stubbornly surviving *Leaves,* expecting that now it would win acclaim and, for a change, even make money.

He was encouraged in his hopes by the first reviews, which were almost all favorable, even touched with praise. Also, the first printing of 2,000 copies were selling steadily, according to the publishers. Whitman could only think happily, at last!

Then came the blow. On March 1, 1882, Osgood and Company received a letter from the District Attorney of Boston. Whitman's book, the Attorney wrote, had been officially classified as obscene. Certain portions of the book must be deleted, the publishers were warned, or they would be prosecuted. At the Attorney's elbow, directing his pen, stood the irate New England Society for the Suppression of Vice.

Whitman, feeling indebted to the publishers, went so far as to agree to deleting a few words or phrases; he did not believe that there could be more than a few that were offensive. When he finally received a long list of changes requested by the District Attorney, including a demand that certain poems be omitted altogether, he saw that compromise was impossible. He rejected the list completely and would not budge from his position.

Osgood, fearful for the reputation of his firm, and unwilling to battle in the courts, recalled the books. Walt was back where he had started from, it seemed.

Whitman wrote of his dismay to Burroughs on April 28th— a dismay augmented by the news that Emerson was dead. He did not know whether he would be able to attend the funeral or not. But what to do about Osgood—could Burroughs lend him one hundred dollars so that he could buy the plates of the book in order to republish the book himself?

Burroughs supplied the needed money (Walt was scrupulous about paying debts), and another old friend rushed forward to help: William O'Connor. The suppression of Whitman's book was too much for the fiery and basically loyal O'Connor. It was an outrage not only to Walt but to literary freedom. Feverishly, O'Connor wrote letters of protest to the newspapers and personally pleaded the cause to anyone and everyone who would listen, determined to face the Attorney General himself. Aroused, O'Connor was a "human avalanche" in Walt's words; "The finest fighter of us all, with the noblest sense of right and justice." As a result of the situation, Whitman and O'Connor were reconciled, and found new pleasure in their companionship.

For Whitman to publish the book himself, in the face of the uproar, would be ruin, O'Connor thought. As it turned out, another publisher, Rees, Walsh and Company of Philadelphia, dared to take over the book. Being "banned in Boston" promoted sales of *Leaves,* and for a year or more it sold so well that Whitman earned around $1,300, a considerable sum to him. The same company brought out his prose work, *Specimen Days,* which also brought in some money, although not as much as Whitman had hoped. Nevertheless, the tide was turning. In the summer of 1883, Bucke's biography was published.

The Staffords had moved from Timber Creek, and Walt was deprived of the rambles he had enjoyed so much there. Other changes, too, were taking place. George decided to leave Camden and move to a small farm he had bought about twelve miles away, at Burlington. He began building a house at the farm and arranged for a special third-floor room for Walt. To George's astonishment, Walt refused to leave Camden with its proximity to the ferries to Philadelphia. The two had a vigorous argument, and for several years George could not forgive his stubborn older brother and refused to see Walt.

The "saintly" Whitman could be as exasperating as anyone else, as even his best friends knew. Mrs. Stafford had experienced his eruptions of temper more than once, although after his angry outbursts had passed, Whitman seemed to forget that he had ever been hot-tempered. Burroughs and O'Connor knew his flaws, his occasional disregard for even the rudiments of common courtesy, his persistent publicizing of himself in the newspapers, his indifference to the time of appointments. But he remained a hero to them. O'Connor and other visitors made their way to a little house on Mickle Street that Whitman bought for himself in March, 1884, raising part of the money from his savings, the rest from a personal loan. The house was a ramshackle one, reverberating with the shuffle of trains only a block away, sullied by soot and coal smoke, but there was a small yard with a tree and a lilac bush, and street cars were only a block away. His furnishings were as drab and spare as usual, wooden boxes serving for extra chairs, a few pans for cooking, a cheap stove for heat. His "study," filled with books and papers, was in a big bed-sitting room on the second floor. Here he entertained visitors, including the English poet and critic, Edmund Gosse. Gosse thought that Camden was one of the grimiest towns he had ever seen and was shocked at Whitman's house. A housekeeper whom Whitman had hired lived in the rooms below him, and she opened the door to Gosse. Then Whitman appeared on the stairs, moving clumsily with the help of his cane, and invited Gosse upstairs to his room—a room with no carpet, a small round stove, one chair, boxes and wall shelves cluttered with objects, mountains of papers in confusion. But the "beautiful old man" was spotlessly clean, and reminded Gosse of "a great old Angora Tom" or perhaps an Oriental sage.

Peter Doyle still visited from time to time, but with less frequency, feeling awkward and inferior in contrast to such erudite persons as Edmund Gosse or the sophisticated and witty Oscar Wilde, who had visited Walt two years earlier.

The housekeeper, a widow, Mrs. Mary Oakes Davis, filled the first floor of the house to overflowing with a dog, a cat, four pet birds, several hens, and an orphan girl she had befriended. Though neighbors may have raised their eyebrows at her living under the same roof with the poet of scandalous fame, it was a matter of economic convenience for both, and Whitman, of course, cared not at all what people said. The important thing was to have someone about who could scrub, cook, and look out for him, which Mrs. Davis did. His lameness was worse and by the spring of 1885 he was all but housebound.

In September of that year, Whitman was delightfully surprised to look out the window of his little house and see a well-groomed horse and an attractive buggy stationed out in front. A lawyer friend, Thomas Donaldson, explained to him that the buggy and horse were a gift from friends, even some who had criticized him, like Whittier. Donaldson had been the instigator of the gift; others who had contributed were Holmes and Mark Twain and the actor, Edwin Booth. The buggy, a phaeton, had been especially built in Columbus, Donaldson told Whitman, and there was money left over from the sum collected for it. He handed Whitman an envelope containing one hundred and thirty-five dollars.

With tears in his eyes, Whitman was helped out to the coach and introduced to the sorrel pony named Frank. From then on, Walt drove wherever he wished with zest—so much so that before long he substituted a peppier horse than Frank. Poor Frank, he had discovered, was groggy in the knees—like Whitman himself.

The white-bearded poet in his phaeton was a familiar sight in Camden. At the same time, his fame was increasing both in his own country and beyond it. The amount of money he earned from his books, however, remained dismally small, and he was still supporting his feeble-minded brother Edward. Friends and supporters helped out in ways that avoided hurting Whitman's pride. Among other things they arranged to continue the annual Lincoln lectures. At the April, 1886, lecture in Philadelphia, a couple of well-wishers paid one hundred dollars each for a ticket, and the manager of the Chestnut Street Opera House donated the use of the hall, so that Whitman received nearly seven hundred dollars for his appearance.

Whitman was realizing his lifetime dream of being a lecturer and being paid far more than he had imagined possible back in the days when he had fitfully seen himself as a traveling poet-preacher charging only a few cents for admission. In May, he received the fifth installment of funds that William Rossetti had been collecting in England; Henry James, who had been so critically severe with Whitman in earlier years, was a contributor.

Throughout his career, Whitman had often had his picture taken at his own expense. Now, photographers, artists, and sculptors were eager to reproduce his likeness, and they came to him with cameras, easels and clay. Foremost among them was Thomas Eakins, a Philadelphia painter and sculptor who was a pioneer in his own field of art and, like Whitman, had felt the lash of critics when they bothered to notice his work at all. Like Whitman, too, he preferred common people and scenes as subjects and painted them in a realistic way. Whitman was one of the few to appreciate Eakins' talent. He said of him, "I never knew of but one artist, and that's Tom Eakins, who could resist the temptation to see what they [people] thought ought to be rather than what is. . . . Eakins is not a painter; he is a force."

Today, Eakins is recognized as one of America's finest painters, and the portrait he did of Whitman is one of his famous works.

Another artist, acclaimed in his own time but generally unknown now, was the popular portrait painter John White Alexander. He sold his painting of Whitman to the Metropolitan Museum in New York, and it hangs there today.

Burroughs still called faithfully, but fretted over his friend's health. Walt ate too much, Burroughs thought, especially fat foods which Burroughs told him clogged and hindered his circulation. Whitman, in turn, worried about O'Connor's health, for O'Connor was visibly failing.

In spite of weakening eyesight—so bad that for a time he feared blindness—Whitman was generally comfortable and content. Although he had passed his peak of inspiration and production, he had not abandoned writing. In his crowded bedroom he mused over the past, the present, and the future. It was the past, however, that held him most now. He kept up what he called his "garrulous notes" and arranged for a new collection of poetry and prose to be called *November Boughs*. This, he thought, would be his last book. He was helped in preparing this collection by a young bank clerk, Horace Traubel, whom Whitman had known in Camden when Traubel was a boy. Traubel was the brother-in-law of another Camden friend, Attorney Thomas Harned. Whitman was a regular Sunday guest at the house of the Harneds, and Traubel was often there, too, intensely interested in Whitman, taking note of all he said, and eager to be of service. He called frequently at Mickle Street and began writing down records of his and Whitman's conversations.

November Boughs was still in preparation on Whitman's sixty-ninth birthday, a day he celebrated at the Harneds'. Several days later, feeling better than usual, he went out in his horse and buggy, driving in the swift fashion he enjoyed. The fresh spring air, the promise of a beautiful sunset, tempted him to linger down by the river where he sat by the water's edge. The air was chilled by the time he got up to leave.

That night Whitman had a second stroke, and for days there was doubt whether he would survive. This doubt was shared by Dr. Bucke who accidentally visited him in early June. Mrs. Davis had been Walt's chief nurse, but she was exhausted by this time, and Dr. Bucke and the famous Philadelphia doctor, William Osler, arranged for a male nurse.

To everyone's surprise, Walt rallied and by July was able to sit in a rocking chair and write a letter to John Burroughs. There were many erasures and words crossed out, but it was reassuring to Burroughs who had been dreading to hear news of Whitman's death. Whitman had not forgotten his plans to print the new book. With Traubel's help he got the manuscript ready for the printer. The new poems were titled "Sands at Seventy"; the prose, *A Backward Glance O'er Travel'd Roads.*

"Here I sit gossiping in the early candle-light of old age," he wrote.

It was not gossip but a thoughtful summing up and re-explanation of why he had written his *Leaves of Grass* and what he had hoped to accomplish through it. "I bid neither for soft eulogies, big money returns, nor the approbation of existing schools and conventions . . . The best comfort of the whole business (after a small band of the dearest friends and upholders ever vouchsafed to man or cause . . .) is that, unstopped and unwarped by any influence outside the soul within me, I have had my say entirely my own way, and put it unerringly on record—the value thereof to be decided by time."

On Whitman's seventieth birthday, his Camden friends arranged a lavish celebration to be held in a hall which they rented. They mailed batches of invitations, and sent notices to critics and well-known authors throughout the world. Whitman was too weak to attend the dinner but was brought to the hall in a new, special wheelchair, to listen to the speeches and telegrams and letters. He, who had suffered years of indifference and attack, was now embarrassed by the extravagant praise he received. On this birthday, he realized also a special desire, the publication of a leather-bound edition of his *Leaves* small enough to fit into a pocket. Although there is little evidence that any of his friends of the working class went around with his book thrust into hip or shirt pocket, he must have hoped that this would be the case.

One long shadow lay over the party, giving a dark edge to Whitman's mood. His friend William O'Connor had died only a couple of weeks before. Anne Gilchrist, too, was gone. Soon it would probably be his turn. What would his seventieth year bring?

> Strength, weakness, blindness, more paralysis and heavier?
> Or placid skies and sun? Wilt thou stir the waters yet?
> Or haply cut me short for good? Or leave me here as now,
> Dull, parrot-like and old, with cracked voice harping,
>   screeching?

11

I Stop Some Where Waiting for You

"He stands a fair chance of outliving us all yet," John Burroughs wrote of Whitman in his "Journal" in September, 1889. He had been to see Walt and found him contentedly sitting in his chair, the familiar wolf skin draped over its back, eating his breakfast of toast and tea, and looking better than he had a year earlier. Throughout a three-hour visit, Walt remained serene, clear, and calm, in the midst of the confusion of his room where even the window shades were torn and crooked.

In good weather, Walt managed short trips outdoors in his wheelchair, propelled by Horace Traubel or a nurse. His life had settled into a quiet pattern of meals, receiving visitors, midday massages, reading the newspapers, jotting in his notebooks, and thinking of still another book.

Traubel was a constant companion, acting as secretary, copyist, errand boy, and interviewer. He pressed, even nagged, Whitman for comments on his past, his beliefs, his feelings, and recorded almost every word or sigh. When he was energetic enough, Whitman would dig into his piles of letters for Traubel, often coming across one from some grateful soldier of the war years. Then, with tears in his eyes, he would listen while Traubel read the letter aloud.

But Whitman was deteriorating steadily, his body racked by more than the effects of his two strokes. Unknown to the doctors attending him, he had widespread tuberculosis affecting several vital organs, bones, his lungs, liver, and stomach. He suffered intense headaches and abdominal distress, so that it is the more amazing that he somehow managed to put on a cheerful look for his visitors and to continue to work. In 1890 he managed, with much assistance, to read his Lincoln lecture once again in April and even to attend another birthday party held in Philadelphia.

But Whitman was preparing for death. Although he at last had enough money to enjoy a few luxuries, he continued to live as frugally as always and to tuck away more and more in savings. Somebody would have to care for poor Eddie, and he meant to see to it that the funds were there. He hoped, also, to leave gifts for friends and to finish a burial vault that he was having built in a Camden cemetery. This was to be a tomb for the Whitman family, its design copied from a drawing by the poet William Blake. He was deceived as to the final cost of the mausoleum. It turned out to be considerably more than he had thought it would be, but he persevered with it.

When, in November of 1890, Jeff died in St. Louis, the burial vault was justified, for Walt could think with comfort of his brother's being buried beside him. Scattered as the family had been in life, restless in their wanderings from house to house, they would all be together again, in the mausoleum. Nevertheless, Jeff's death, from a lingering and unspecified disease, was a painful shock to Walt. He wrote Jeff's obituary for the *Engineering Record* and in his poetry faced the approaching shadow of his own death while he composed still another preface for his forthcoming book of poetry and prose, *Good-bye My Fancy*.

Had I not better withhold (in this old age and paralysis of me) such little tags and fringe-dots (maybe specks, stains) as follow a long, dusty journey, and witness it afterward? . . . Though not at all clear that, as here collated, it is worth printing (certainly I have nothing fresh to write) —I while away the hours of my 72nd year—hours of forced confinement in my den—by putting in shape this small old age collation:

Last droplets of and after spontaneous rain,
From many limpid distillations and past showers;
(Will they germinate anything? mere exhalations as they
      all are—the land's and sea's—America's;
Will they filter to any deep emotion? any heart and brain?)

However that may be, I feel like improving today's opportunity and wind up.

The pain-racked, dying poet could still respond to the "sunny-fine" days of July. "Old as I am I feel today almost a part of some frolicsome wave, or for sporting yet like a kid or kitten . . ." Yet, he is only an old "shell-fish," he knows. But there were those moments when he still felt a streak of physical perfection. "I believe I have it in me perennially anyhow." With now almost no lungs left with which to breathe!

The book came out in 1891. Even this was not enough. The tinkering and rearranging of the *Leaves* continued. After eight editions there must still be one more. In December, 1891, Whitman had a few advance copies of this final edition bound as Christmas presents for friends. This was a two-volume edition, dated 1892, which included *November Boughs* and *Good-bye My Fancy*. It also included *An Executor's Diary Note,* in which he recognized that this *was* his last arrangement of his book, one which should not be tampered with by any future editor. Called the "death bed edition," this is the one from which anthologists quote.

In late December, Traubel wrote to Burroughs that Whitman was nearing the end. Burroughs hurried to Camden. He found Walt in bed, weak and feebly coughing, but able to talk and to hand him a copy of the specially bound *Leaves*. Walt's brother George had just been there, and Walt felt quite emotional about the visit.

Burroughs was still in Camden on Christmas Day, surprised and relieved to find Walt seemingly better, his voice strong and natural as he talked of Ellen O'Connor, Eldridge, and other friends. Even better than the doctors, Whitman knew he was dying. To Burroughs he looked pathetic, but beautiful.

Although resigned to death, ready for it, Whitman fought for life, his spirit stronger than the flesh, and in February he was still able to write a last message to his friends. "Well, I must send you all, dear fellows, a word from my own hand, propped up in bed, deadly weak, but the spark seems to glimmer yet . . . Again I repeat, my thanks to you . . . Goodbye to all." Traubel and Harned lithographed the message and sent it out to Walt's friends in both the United States and England.

To him, in turn, came letters and cables almost every day, and he managed to dictate replies. Though in great pain much of the time, he did not complain. However, toward the end of March, he began to yearn for that "lovely and soothing death" he had described in his elegy for President Lincoln.

Death came quietly to Whitman on the evening of March 26, 1892. A gentle rain was falling to glisten on the thickening buds of the lilac bush in the backyard below. Whitman was conscious to the last, and calm, his right hand resting in one of Horace Traubel's.

John Burroughs was benumbed. The black crepe on the door bell of the little Mickle Street house, the closed shutters, seemed as unreal as the mortal remains of Whitman in his coffin. It was Walt and yet it was not. Walt had believed firmly in the immortality of the soul. Burroughs could not, but he found himself in communion with Walt's spirit, addressing him mentally as if Walt could still hear and understand. And although Burroughs had known his "great friend" for so many years, familiar with his eccentricities and flaws, after Walt's death he felt, in his excess of grief, that Whitman was actually "the Christ of the modern world"—redeeming it and justifying it with human-divine love.

On the day of the funeral, March 30th, several thousand men and women went through the Mickle Street house to view the coffin. Among them was Peter Doyle, one of the many "dear comrades" Walt had loved. At the cemetery, too, there was a huge crowd. The services were held in a large tent perfumed with flowers. Burroughs, listening to the funeral oration, remembered a night when he and Walt had watched together the glorious migration of birds across the night-dark sky, hearing the wing rustle and occasional song of the bobolinks, tanagers, thrushes and plovers passing over. Now he heard above the funeral tent the warble of a bluebird. The warble seemed joyous, welcoming the spring and all the pleasures of blossom, fruit, and harvest that Walt had so loved and celebrated to almost the final moment of consciousness.

> Beginning my studies the first step pleased me so much,
> The mere fact consciousness, these forms, the power of motion,
> The least insect or animal, the senses, eyesight, love,

The first step I saw awed me and pleased me so much,
I have hardly gone and hardly wished to go any farther,
But stop and loiter all the time to sing it in ecstatic songs.

It is over a hundred years since Whitman published his first thin edition of *Leaves of Grass* containing twelve poems. From the time of its publication, 1855, to the final edition, 1892, the twelve poems had grown to nearly four hundred—not counting some thirty poems which he rejected as imperfect. This is a tremendous amount of work, particularly when one considers all the other writing Whitman did as journalist, editor, chronicler of times and events, critic, social commentator, diarist, letter writer, author of long prefaces, and the books *Specimen Days* and *Democratic Vistas*.

He used the phrase "my omnivorous lines" in one of his poems to describe such outpouring of words, declaring that he "must not write any less." At his death, he had indeed left a "wonderful and ponderous" work behind him, a vibrant testament to his energy, his dedication, and his genius.

Against those who consider Whitman America's greatest poet, there are some who berate not only his poetry but consider the man himself a sham. Even admirers of Whitman acknowledge that he was by no means modest and that he in some ways did tend to "play up" the role of the Great American Bard, prophet, and even savior. But if his admirers are correct, and they are well in the majority, he *is* the great American bard. In regard to prophecy, he was right more often than he was wrong. As for being a savior, this role was attributed to Whitman by over-adoring friends, not something that he seriously claimed for himself. Yet, in the fetid wards of the Civil War hospitals where Whitman exhausted himself caring for the sick and wounded, the "good gray poet" with his embracing compassion and charity, must often have seemed almost a saint to helpless and hopeless soldiers.

Regardless of all this, the important matter is Whitman's poetry. What about those four hundred poems that are his legacy? Is each and every one a masterpiece? Of course not, and not even Whitman's most zealous defenders would claim this. There are, in fact, many lines, and even many poems, that are badly flawed or simply dull. Although he fought against sentimentality, it sometimes cropped up in his work. And though he resisted the flowery kind of utterances typical of his time, he fell into the flower trap more than once. Those who strain toward the heights have the farthest to fall, and when Whitman fell it could be with a resounding thud. In this he was no different from all poets, artists, composers, or other creators before and after him.

So, the truly important thing is the achievement, and Whitman's achievement was, and is, momentous. Without his magnificent elegy to Lincoln, alone, American literature would be vastly impoverished. The same can be said of other great poems he wrote: "Out of the Cradle Endlessly Rocking," "Song of Myself" (with its numerous self-contained poems included in the over-all structure), "Passage to India," "Song of the Open Road," "Song of Occupations," or "I Sing the Body Electric."

He wrote of his work, ". . . a book I have made, The words of my book nothing, the drift of it everything."

But the drift had to be expressed in words, and was, regardless of Whitman's own disclaimer. He also said, "Speech is the twin of my vision." This vision, this "drift," and Whitman's own personality were, of course, inseparable from his poetry. The poems are autobiographical, but they also contain the multiple voice of America itself at a time when to be an American was to believe that one was a member of a new race, and that the "common man" especially was the new nobility. The terms "democracy" and "independence" had an almost religious aura in the years when many persons could still remember the war against the British. Whitman carried the concept of democracy beyond physical frontiers, lifting it into a cosmic realm. Human brotherhood, too, was transmuted by his imagination into a mystic, universal love.

For him, everything was a particle of the divine, everything contained a mystery, from the "mossy scabs of the worm fence, heaped stones, elder, mullein and poke weed" to "a leaf of grass."

> I believe a leaf of grass is no less than the journeywork of
>   the stars,
> And the pismire is equally perfect, and a grain of sand,
>   and the egg of the wren,
> And the tree-toad is a chef-d'oeuvre for the highest,
> And the running blackberry would adorn the parlors of
>   heaven,
> And the narrowest hinge in my hand puts to scorn all machinery,
> And the cow crunching with depressed head surpasses any
>   statue,
> And a mouse is miracle enough to stagger sextillions of
>   infidels,
> And I could come every afternoon of my life to look at the
>   farmer's girl boiling her iron tea-kettle and baking
>   shortcake.

Dozens of books and articles have been devoted to what Whitman said or thought or might have thought, and each year more is added to the growing bibliography. The popular poets of Whitman's time—Longfellow, Whittier, Lowell, Holmes—seem like tintype figures in fading albums by comparison with Walt. Whitman, "one of the roughs," is still grandly alive, speaking to poets of our time—Hart Crane, Garcia Lorca, Allen Ginsberg, Ezra Pound—his voice carrying a modern ring. Between 1945 and 1960 there were some thirty-seven editions of his poetry, prose, and letters published. A list of the foreign translations of his work would take almost a page in itself; it would include editions in Chinese, Hebrew, Czechoslovakian, Norwegian, Spanish, and Russian. His name crops up often in book reviews, and his burial vault is a mecca for literary-minded tourists. Even the spring at Timber Creek where he wrote and bathed now displays a New Jersey historical marker, with pilgrimages to the area arranged by the Walt Whitman Society. The same Society, in 1967, began seeking funds to restore Whitman's last dwelling place, the old house on Mickle Street, Camden, which had fallen into a dreary state of disrepair.

Poorly educated, struggling most of his life to make a bare living, sentimentalist and mystic, politician and poet, rude and saintly, self-publicist but tireless servant of the sick and wounded, Whitman contained the multitudes of contradictions he claimed for himself. If he is still not understood completely, it is not surprising, for genius is seldom simple, and Walt Whitman was a genius.

His own words remain the best clue to his poetry: "The reader will always have his or her part to do, just as much as I have mine. I seek less to state or display any theme or thought, and more to bring you, reader, into the atmosphere of the theme or thought—there to pursue your own flight."

> I depart as air . . . . I shake my white locks at the runaway
>   sun,
> I effuse my flesh in eddies, and drift it in lacy jags.

I bequeath myself to the dirt to grow from the grass I love,
If you want me again look for me under your bootsoles.

You will hardly know who I am or what I mean,
But I shall be good health to you nevertheless,
And filter and fibre your blood.

Failing to fetch me at first keep encouraged,
Missing me one place search another,
I stop some where waiting for you.

Selected Bibliography

Allen, Gay Wilson, *The Solitary Singer*. New York, The Macmillan Co., 1955.

Barrus, Clara, *Walt Whitman and Burroughs Comrades*. Boston, Houghton Mifflin Co., 1931.

Bucke, Richard Maurice, Harned, Thomas B., and Traubel, Horace L., eds., *The Complete Writings of Walt Whitman,* 10 vols., New York and London, 1902.

Canby, Henry Seidel, *Walt Whitman, An American*. Boston, Houghton Mifflin Co., 1943.

Gohdes, Clarence and Silver, Rollo G., eds., *Faint Clews & Indirections: Manuscripts of Walt Whitman and His Family,* Durham, North Carolina, Duke University Press, 1949.

Harned, Thomas B., ed., *Letters of Anne Gilchrist to Walt Whitman,* New York, Doubleday, Page & Co., 1918.

Miller, Edwin H., ed., *The Collected Writings of Walt Whitman,* Vol. I, New York, New York University Press, 1966.

Whitman, Walt, *Complete Poetry and Selected Prose,* James E. Miller, Jr., ed., Riverside Press. Boston, Houghton Mifflin Co., 1959.

Whitman, Walt, *Leaves of Grass*. Reprint of first edition published in Brooklyn, New York, 1855. Dolphin Books. New York, Doubleday & Co., Inc., 1966.

Whitman, Walt, *Specimen Days*. Signet Classics. New York, The New American Library of World Literature, Inc., 1961.

177

Whitman, Edward (defective brother of Walt), 35, 43, 62, 78, 111, 123, 125, 135, 139, 165

Whitman, George Washington (brother of Walt), 10, 13, 17, 87, 117, 122, 125, 127, 135, 136, 140, 141, 147, 157-158, 167
Civil War volunteer, 77, 78-79, 80-81, 96-97, 98, 99-100
comment by, on *Leaves of Grass,* 54
Walt characterized by, 37, 40

Whitman, Hannah (sister of Walt), 2, 13, 35, 87

Whitman, Jesse (brother of Walt), 2, 13, 35, 74, 78, 92, 93
commitment of, to lunatic asylum, 97, 98
death of, 124

Whitman, Jesse (grandfather of Walt, Jr.), 3

Whitman, Louisa ("Lou," wife of George), 127, 135, 136, 140, 147

Whitman, Louisa (mother of Walt), 7, 10, 35, 43, 78, 79, 92, 111, 123, 125
attitude of, toward Walt, 13, 61-62
death of, 135
health of, 10, 127
letters to Walt from, 93, 124
reaction of, to *Leaves of Grass,* 54, 87
Walt's description of, 3, 11, 87, 135

Whitman, Martha ("Matty," wife of Jeff), 85, 92
death of, 134, 135

Whitman, Mary (sister of Walt), 4, 13, 35, 37

Whitman, Thomas Jefferson (Jeff, brother of Walt), 10, 13, 25, 78, 85, 87, 92, 93, 111, 117, 125, 134, 146, 151, 152, 153
death of, 165
Walt's companion on New Orleans venture, 29-33

Whitman, Walt
biography of, by Bucke, 157
birth of, 1
brothers and sisters of, 10, 13, 61
See also individual family names
characterizations of, 25, 38, 86-87, 92, 116
Civil War activities of, 81-83, 84-92, 95-96, 100, 133, 163
as a compositor, 11-12
critics' attacks on, 73-74
critics' praise of, 74
death of, 167
description of, 10, 67, 86, 88, 146
dismissal of, from government job, 112
earliest poems of, 35
editorial jobs held by, 21, 22, 25, 28, 31-32, 34-35, 36, 62, 3
evaluation of, as a poet, 169-173
failing eyesight of, 161
family responsibilities of, 74, 78, 111, 116, 123
first published stories by, 19-20
funeral of, 168
government jobs held by, 85, 98, 113
health of, 88, 90, 92, 95, 96, 97, 122, 123, 127, 165
homosexuality of, in question, 59
horse-and-buggy gift to, 159
late poems of, 137-138, 139